SIX MEN ON A WALK

But We forgot the dog.

Iain Jackson
Illustrations by James Pilcher

Published by Iain Jackson
Publishing partner: Paragon Publishing, Rothersthorpe

ISBN 978-1-899820-54-2
Book design, layout and production management by Into Print
www.intoprint.net
Printed and bound in UK and USA by Lightning Source

Illustrations by James Pilcher

With thanks to:

Alison and Fiona for their patience, tolerance and support of my obsession with the outdoors.

Fergus for being prepared to stick to my walking pace at all times (Yes I am aware he was on a lead).

Tosca for not objecting too much when left behind on all those lovely long walks.

With Apologies to:

Mark Dickins for the number of times in this book he is viewed with both envy and derision for his ability to disappear over the horizon apparently without effort.

Paul Martin for all the unjust references in this book to his love of food and associated BMI.

Tony Kennedy as he is not at all in reality like a Labrador puppy.

John Milner who is certainly not old enough to be my Dad

And James Pilcher. Actually James is such a nice bloke I don't think I found a single opportunity to be rude about him but just in case I'll apologise anyway.

The Idea

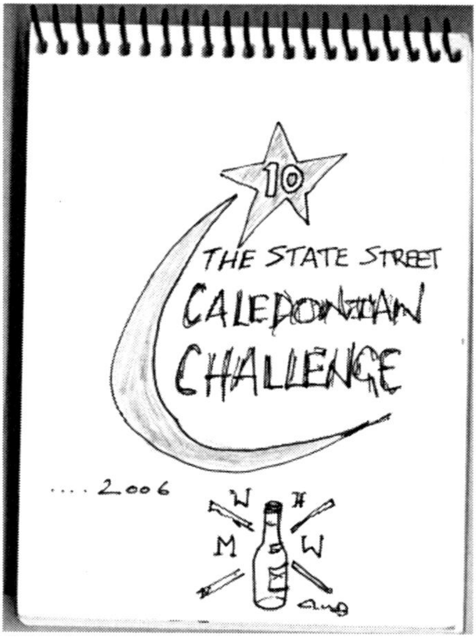

Like all the best ideas this one started in the pub. Yes it probably is a symptom of a mid-life crisis, our generation of mostly forty something's almost embarrassingly refuses to accept the consequences of ageing and hangs on to a pursuit of sport long after we should be concentrating on bridge or chess as active pursuits.

I am not, and probably never will be, capable of completing the route of the Tour de France or the Hawaii Ironman triathlon as an outlet for all of this frustrated energy but the Caledonian Challenge sounded possible. Tough enough to be intimidating but not impossible, 54 miles of the West Highland Way completed within twenty four hours must be achievable, mustn't it?

After all, even allowing for stops, 54 miles in twenty hours of walking is only 2.7 miles per hour which is about the speed one strolls home from the pub. Aside from all of that the event was in June of the next year which in a year's time was far enough away for any reality to be incidental. So armed with several large malts and more calculations concluding on how 17 hours would be a good target for completion the "Gravesend Windmill Hill Scottish Malt

Whisky Society" signed up for the Caledonian Challenge. Actually the genesis of this idea wasn't mine. Paul had some colleagues who had completed it the year before ("fairly" easy was the alleged summary of the event) and since we had in the whisky club talked many times about a visit to Scotland this seemed liked the ideal excuse to hang a trip on. Somehow, and I must admit I'm not really sure how, it is a more legitimate excuse to selfishly spend time purely on yourself when linked to some tangible event.

I can't explain why but the Caledonian Challenge was always likely to meet a higher family approval rating than a lad's weekend in Scotland involving distillery tours, golf and drinking, but it was and it did.

The idea might have remained just that. As grumpy middle aged men we do seem to specialise in moaning rather than doing. In fact if there were an Olympic medal available for recreational grumbling I reckon GWHSMWS might well be up for the gold.

However the rest of the whisky club reckoned without me. I have a long track record of ailing madness in these matters, my track record stemming back to completing the Lyke Wake Walk in the sixth form and continuing through various hill walking and adventure racing events. I've never understood why I am so keen as I'm the fattest endurance athlete in Britain. (Athlete is not the right word but the only one I could find, there isn't a good word in English for me perhaps we could settle for fatlete?) I am always at the back of the pack. Hill walking with my brother mostly consists of observing him as a speck in the distance. Actually it doesn't have to be my brother; it's the same deal whenever I walk in the hills. You probably know the drill. Just as I arrive at the top of the steepest slope sweating profusely and breathing mostly through my backside I find

the rest of the assembled party are slinging their rucksacks over their shoulder having just partaken of a three course lunch with a nice glass of claret and cheerfully announcing "Time we pressed on then!"
Somehow it has never dampened my enthusiasm for taking on challenges I am so obviously unsuited for. More than that, I am often the driving force and spiritual if not physical leader of them. I latched immediately onto the idea of the Caledonian Challenge - to me it seemed perfect, difficult enough to be really challenging but clearly not impossible. In management bollocks parlance I decided to go for the presumptive close (sounds good no idea what it means though).

June 05 from Iain to whisky club

One other idea if we want to really do it on the cheap. Drive up in my car (free petrol insured for all drivers) on Friday, camp Friday night and Saturday and then stay somewhere more civilized Sunday evening after partaking of enormous quantity of beer and whisky. Drive home Monday. You absolutely need a driver for the event you can't carry all the needed gear for a 24 hour walk and if someone drops out you need a vehicle to rescue them. The driver should meet you at every check point with food, clean and spare clothes and lots of encouragement. I agree it's a very boring job.
The important part of this is commitment starting with a commitment we are going to do it everything else is just details. My proposal is we send a note to all whisky club members asking for definites, maybes, potential drivers, and those in the "you must be joking" but I might come to Scotland to laugh category. In my

```
view we should do it now, if we wait like so
many other plans it will fizzle out, family will
book holiday, work will book a trip to Japan,
swimming will book a critical Gala, family
will tell you it's Dad's birthday, or you have
to collect daughter from University or some
other equally important event that weekend and
it will never happen. I am happy to make sure I
track web site and enter at least one team as
soon as it opens for next year.
Are you in???
Iain
```

We had a clearly assembled a group where the ability to complete the challenge was in inverse proportion to the enthusiasm for doing it. Paul who had originally sparked the whole thing was by far the most enthused but also at this stage the least fit. If not quite as heavy as me he was at least as rotund and did far less exercise. Mark by contrast who was as fit as a butchers dog was a go with the flow specialist and didn't have email anyway so would never be likely to reply. As expected Paul replied almost immediately.

```
I am unequivocally in. Cheap is good but if we
plan far enough in advance we should be able
to ensure value for money. However protracted
it may become we ought to throw it open to the
rest of the WC to get immediate commitment
(barring death - can't expect people to turn up
if their dead) give people the in or out option.
I personally like the driving up idea (free
petrol!!, can I borrow your car every weekend?)
- This will ensure cheap travel, we will have a
support car and I don't mind driving up (IJ I
know you drive all the time and are not keen but
the rest of the team can shoulder it).
```

I'm looking forward to the Cally Challenge already - James and i have already started training with a 16 mile bike ride on Sunday morning, which involved a thigh breaking trip up Taylors lane, up Villa Rd and Pear Tree lane.

If we can get one team confirmed quickly, which I think we can, then the other can follow, if indeed it does.

Paul Martin
Charles Taylor Consulting

I knew we should just go for it. I was absolutely convinced that apart from John and me no one else had the faintest idea of what they were letting themselves in for. It reminded me so much of a conversation at work with two girls about to embark on the three peaks challenge of climbing Ben Nevis, Sca fell Pike and Snowdon in twenty four hours. I was originally planning to do it but had prolapsed a disc and had to drop out. About a week before departing I casually enquired about their training progress. After a couple of rather quizzical looks they offered up the answer that they had been taking the dog to walk in the park regularly.
I've not to date climbed Ben Nevis but I have done about 50 other Scottish mountains and they have all been tough. Those that know about these things assure me Ben Nevis by the tourist path is an un-remitting slog and a walk in the park it definitely is not. Until you've actually done it it is very hard to imagine what it is like to walk steeply uphill for hours at a time. It doesn't extrapolate well from any normal activity and you have to experience it to feel it. With a week to go advice was useless anyway there is nothing helpful you can do a week before an event like this.

To their credit they both sumitted Ben Nevis although Sca Fell and Snowdon proved beyond them. I should also mention they took about seven hours to get up and down Ben Nevis against a target time of around four and a half hours.
I seriously wondered if were heading the same way. Self delusion becomes easier as you get older and I really started to doubt we could do it. Still we had eight months to prepare and we certainly weren't going to find out if we could do it by sitting in Gravesend so time to get started, well entered at least.

From: Iain Jackson [mailto:ijackson@lsil.com]
Sent: 29 June 2005 13:58
To: David Lewis; James Pilcher; Paul Martin (E-mail); Tony Kennedy (E-mail); Stewart Owen; b.king(E-mail); john.milner(E-mail); Iain Jackson
Subject: Invite

All (James can you deliver paper copy to Laurence & Mark, Tony can you deliver paper copy to Andy)
As mooted first by the slightly mad Paul Martin and then joined with gusto by the terminally insane Mr. Iain Jackson the **Gravesend Windmill Hill Scottish Malt Whisky Society** is committed to entering a team (or teams) to the "Caledonian Challenge" a 54 mile walk across Glencoe and Rannoch Moor down the West Highland Way for June 2006. The walk is to be completed as a continuous walk within 24 hours starting at 7am on a Saturday and finishing before 7am Sunday. You now have enough information to enter if you want more details check out http://www.caledonianchallenge.com/ for the full SP especially the section on "personal

preparation". (http://www.caledonianchallenge.com/event/prepare.php). The exact weekend isn't known yet but it will be in June next year. Please let me and Paul M. know your interest by selecting one of the following categories.

1. I'm definitely doing it. (Acts of God, flood, fire and pestilence permitting)

2. I might do it (this means you're interested but until you change to category (1) we won't add an additional team on your behalf nor plan travel or accommodation. Pot luck on fitting you in depending on when you change from (1) to (2)).

3. I'd be prepared to be a support driver. (Involves meeting the team at various check points with supplies and dry clothes and is not a great job since you have to hang around a lot and stay up until 4 am, each team **has** to have a support driver though).

4. Not bloody likely although I might come to Scotland for the weekend for the crack.

5. I don't travel North of Watford Gap.

Inspiration and ***intimidation*** available in equal measure from the attached image of the WHW snaking across Rannoch Moor.

```
Let me know your thoughts by the end of July. No
reply puts you down as a Softie Southerner in
category (5).
Iain
```

Of course email confirmation can only take you so far. What we really needed was commitment, and long experience tells me that at least the early commitment is most easily obtained. Later judgement is seriously flawed through the taking of far too much drink!

Drink is a very wonderful thing, but as we would say a bit of a double edged sword. Frankly speaking even the government can't make up its mind since it continually tells us not to drink more than 27 units a week and runs campaigns against binge drinking and at the same time opens pubs up 24 hours a day. Have these guys never had a drink? Don't they realise that most people who have had too much to drink by 1 am will continue to drink until 2 am if the opportunity presents itself?

Another thing that really gets my goat is the idea that 27 units is the exact recommended maximum consumption whether you are a seven stone weakling who does no exercise at all or a 20 stone international rugby forward at the peak of his physical prowess. It's clearly rubbish. Last time I looked the human race was pretty diverse and had a huge spectrum of responses to most stimuli including alcohol. That's a concept much too difficult for a government to deal with much better to assume we are all identical and set "targets" that apparently apply equally to all, madness.

Anyway enough of the grumpy middle aged man ranting. The point for the whisky club and the Caledonian Challenge was to sell the concept at the next meeting over a few large malts.

This is where my own troubles usually start. As a general rule I love whisky, always neat and usually pretty hefty measures. Normally though it is only a last drink of the evening or one or two after a dinner party and the "hefty" measure element can be survived without major disfunctionality. Whisky club evening is a different matter altogether since the main purpose of the evening is to taste (or rather drink) several different whisky's. My grandfather always maintained a single pub measure was not enough to wet the glass. By contrast a single whisky club measure could safely arrest a heard of stampeding buffalo by simply waving it in their general direction.

Our summer meeting was scheduled pretty soon and as usual involved a number of stupid pub challenges (darts, hoopla, mini golf if I remember correctly, which I assuredly don't) and a certain large number of malts.

Enthusiasm for the undertaking increased in proportion to the number of malts consumed and by the end of the

evening we had at least seven confirmed walkers.
Of course some of them probably wouldn't remember their commitment the next day but in a typically annoying way, even in my state of highest inebriation, I would make sure those that signed up would be entered.
I really do have a love hate relationship with whisky. There are times when a long draft of a really fine single malt tastes like the best thing in the world. It's such a complex flavour, and so varied. Smooth and soft, a 25 year old Macallan for me or a deep complex oily seaweedy flavour like a Lagavulin or a Laphroaig. My brother swears by a Brora (extinct distillery; allegedly the 1972 vintage has the highest phenol content of any malt) and I had a present once of a bottle of "The Family Silver" that was the best thing I've ever tasted. Trouble is The Family Silver was a generic brand for a selection of rare malts and I can't remember which distillery mine was from. Pity.
The down side is of course the compulsion to drink more. I've never ever fancied a drink in the morning and I rarely drink at lunchtime, save the occasional pint when on holiday but when I start drinking whisky I also don't know when to stop. A strange behaviour I can't totally explain and one that is only arrested by the simple act of not starting very often. Boy what a marketing man's dream though a product that when you start drinking it you just want to keep going. Shame about the down sides but overall I'll live with it. The world would be a much poorer place without the rich complexity and diversity that is Scottish Malt Whisky. Just ponder that you can produce all of that diverse range of tastes and aromas from just barley, water and yeast, truly amazing.
The next few days were a time for a more sober assessment of what we were signing up for.

Of course sobriety brought some reasoning into the calculations, 54 miles is a mighty long way and the last time I drove over Rannoch Moor (in August this year), which is about half way along the walk, my car temperature gauge read 9°C, and it was raining. Actually I've driven over Rannoch Moor many times and it is always raining. On the same day it was 26°C in Gravesend, so some reality checking was in order.

I did offer some further calibration, the last time I attempted something like this was in 1997 when a group from work (me included) completed the 24 peaks, a round of 24 Lake District summits completed in 24 hours, a mere beginners effort at 32 miles. We did finish it but along the way one of our crew managed to fill his boots with blood leaking from various nasty burst blisters, rubbing boots, and over the course of the few days after the event shed several toe nails. Carpet slippers were the order of the day as footwear for at least a couple of weeks afterwards; for all of us, not just the guy with mangled feet!

My memory is not great but I also had vivid memories of completing the Lyke Wake Walk when in the sixth form. The Lyke Wake Walk is 42 miles across the north Yorkshire Moors to be completed within a single twenty four hour period. I can relive to this day the instant a blister on the sole of my foot burst. I haven't ever walked on hot coals but it felt like someone had stuck a red hot needle in my foot. I also remember vividly that it pissed it down for the last few hours, and when we got back to our camp site my tent had floated away and I slept the night on the bench of the school mini bus.

So why would I want to go through this again? Aged forty four and with two prolapsed discs behind me, it seemed I might finally be losing my marbles.

Clearly what was needed was a structured training program; start slowly, build up to longer and longer walk that sort of thing. It's best not to start too soon though, so for now I simply entered the team. A £100 pound commitment per person was paid and so there we were entered, no going back now.

The team (you'll get to know them better as time moves on):

- James: 45, stick thin, hockey player, fit;
- Mark: 44, still playing good football, irritatingly fit without seeming to try. Once ran a marathon measured by his mates in the car in 3hour 45 minutes after a bet with the same mates in the pub the night before;
- Tony: 44, Northern, small, unbelievably positive and hyperactive like next doors Labrador puppy who escaped into your garden;
- Paul: 40, determined as hell, fitness doubtful, dodgy knee;
- John: a youngster so we don't mention his age, another Northerner, quietly confident;
- David: 44, reserve at the time of booking, possessor of the best golf swing of anyone I've ever played with, plays of 3 off about three games a year. Fitness pedigree an unknown. (Dropped out before first training walk citing injury and eventually disappeared without trace);
- Fergus: 6, a soft coated wheaten terrier of doubtful brain power, with a manic personality especially in the vicinity of cats;
- And me, Iain (Jacko): 44, self appointed team leader, irritatingly dogmatic and opinionated, reasonably fit (played rugby for years averagely) but also quite fat (18stone + at the last count)!

Starting to "Train"

Fast forward a bit to October. Nothing had really happened since we entered in the summer but with the onset of autumn the time was coming where we really needed to start. At least start getting into people's heads the difficulty of the task ahead which hopefully would precipitate some action. Goals are useless unless they motivate some change to what you do. It drives me crazy in business when people around and above me slip into "Management by hopeful outcome" mode. A classic example: my boss (based in California) rings me in my capacity as head of European marketing. He begins "You know Iain I've been thinking (unlikely I ponder) that what we need to do is make our top customer a $50 million account for us". That was it: simple really, just make them a $50 million account and life will be good. No mention or discussion of what we should actually **do,** just a simple statement of what should happen. By itself I assumed, or maybe by magic. It wasn't like we weren't already investing huge time and effort in the account already. The really frustrating aspect was that he wasn't asking me to deploy extra resource on the account, or to deploy a newly developed product strategy, or to garner extra engineering resource to work on some new products – no, he simply told me what the outcome should be. Useless.

MBHO sits right up there with my other favourite technique - "third choice" management.
Choice 1: The project can be completed in six months and will cost 1 million dollars
Choice 2: The project can be completed in three months

and will cost 1.5 million dollars and there is a 20-30% chance we will miss the schedule.
Management response is to test the assumptions used to create choices 1&2 and having fully convinced themselves the reasoning is sound and the assumptions valid they then create (the unavailable) choice 3 which they impose on the team and represent to their management as their value add.
Choice 3: The project is guaranteed to take less than three months and will cost less than 800 thousand dollars.
Brilliant.

The same threatened to be true of our CC walk. We all really wanted to do it, and most could probably visualise the satisfaction of finishing, but the reality was we hadn't taken even the smallest step to prepare ourselves.
We were all collectively in danger of subscribing to our own choice three which went something like "I'll do bare minimum (or no) training and then I'll breeze round 54 miles in seventeen hours and be finished in time for last orders"
Well we had to start somewhere, and by pure chance the appointed host for the October whisky club meet (Stewart, a non-walker) had to drop the proposed whisky and Scaletrix meeting and so I jumped in to propose a lengthy pub crawl. Well at least lengthy in comparison to most pub crawls even if still minuscule in comparison to the actual CC walk itself.
A simple enough excursion, Christine kindly dropped us by "The Railway" in Sole Street where we promptly stopped for a pint of course. John was a bit gobsmacked when we started walking all of ten minutes later having bought and consumed our various pints in fairly smart time. It was, it has to be said, his first ever whisky meeting and without the

benefit of recent rugby tours (or similar acts of stupendous alcoholic over indulgence) he probably couldn't reasonably be expected to anticipate the volume of alcohol involved in a regular GWHSMWS meeting. A short 1km later and we were ensconced in The Cock at Luddesdowne. I really rate this pub; no gastro pub here, this is a proper pub not a crap restaurant masquerading as a pub. It also sells the best beer in the area and well worth a visit. Suitably enthused by the excellent beer we had to stop here for a couple (editors note: a couple is a generic term intending to broadly describe anywhere between two and six beers). Onwards to Cobham, a 3km stroll on various footpaths.

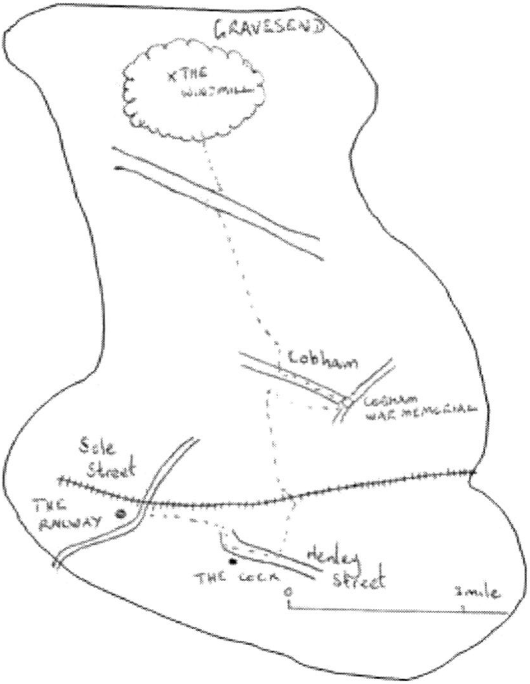

Our continued embarrassing refusal to act our age was compounded by the walk having to stop at Cobham war memorial to complete the annual Club Conker Championship, during the course of which of course we completed some whisky “tasting”. It would have made an interesting conversation if PC Plod had stopped by whilst seven middle aged blokes played conkers and downed large malts in the middle of Cobham village. Yob culture gone mad I hear them cry.

The final leg to The Windmill unfortunately involved a tedious walk back through Gravesend. This part of course was completed very speedily as we raced back to the pub before closing. The landlord has never had such welcome customers as we proceeded to drink most of his bottle of Balvenie and a not inconsequential amount of Glenmorangie. By the way, the Windmill is also an excellent pub serving beer and food of note whilst retaining the character of a proper English pub.

Lawrence, one of our most loyal members and confirmed non walker, decided on the very rational plan of meeting us in The Windmill. Sadly whilst the plan was rational, we were not by the time of his arrival at 10pm. The approximate round of drinks he got landed with was three Green King IPA, two Stella's, three London Pride and eight large Balvenie's. So for the very doubtful privilege of spending an hour in the company of his drunken mates he parted company with the best part of fifty quid. Bargain.

John's email of the next day was totally not fair; I have no recollection at all of buying him a treble!

On Sat morning I had two injuries. A very sore head which I knew was coming when I got double vision and couldn't speak properly (Iain I think the treble may have nailed me), and a big conkering bruise on my inner wrist.

A great night. Look forward to round two later this month.
Regards
John

John Milner APMP MRICS
Partner
For and on behalf of Baily Garner LLP

At this time we were definitely at the stage of unreasonable optimism about the whole endeavour. Perhaps a stroll back from the pub is a bit of an optimistic comparison to 54 miles of Scottish bog but we really believed we could do it. The more beer and whisky we drank the more we believed we could do it. Great stuff this drink - **GAME ON**!
As I told you before we were all committed to this, right? Well middle aged enthusiasm does come with some baggage; not least, all of us have families that quite rightly command priority attention, followed by the need to stay in gainful employment and pay the mortgage. So with the best will in the world, training for the Caledonian Challenge could only be at best priority three and sure enough when it came to our first proper training walk attendance was a bit thin. Strange though that the first "pub crawl" effort yielded seven out of eight (Fergus didn't walk on account of his unsuitability for imbibing whisky) but for the first training walk we were down to four (including Fergus) and two half's.
The walk was split as a first bit of four miles including all dogs and families who wanted to participate and a second loop of six miles for "serious" walkers. The first loop yielded nine adults, four children and five dogs, and just getting everyone out of the door was like trying to herd cats. A serious sense of humour failure on my part followed

but eventually everyone rounded up missing hats, gloves, boots, dogs and water bottles; someone at one point even mislaid their other half, who was found sitting in the car outside, but we eventually got going. We convened in the car park at Trosley Country Park ready for our first proper "expedition". I almost felt proud.

Of our walking team only James, Paul, Fergus and I made the whole trip (ten miles). Tony and John made only the short first loop due to unavoidable family conflicts, and Mark (playing footie) and David (poorly) missed out altogether.

As mentioned before, Mark is so irritatingly fit it won't matter from a fitness point of view if he never joins a training walk, but training now would be useful later from a team spirit point of view. We weren't ever going to be the fittest or fastest bunch so it was vital we created a sense of team spirit and aimed to help each other along with a sense of common purpose.

Starting about 2:30 we sauntered along the top of the North Downs Way. After about 150m, Tony (pathologically positive person as I told you) declared this to be "all right" and asked me for the first time whether the pace was about right for the Caledonian Challenge. In the next six months Tony would pose the same question approximately every twenty minutes when walking with him. Well I guess it was a relevant issue but extrapolating a 150m of flat walking to 54 miles of the West Highland Way was something of a challenge even for my hyperactive imagination. The walk passed off peacefully if slowly and we finished the first part at about 4:30pm with a splinter group of me James and Tony sprinting back to the car park to avoid the cars being locked in overnight.

Two miles an hour won't win any races but the kids and especially the dogs enjoyed their romp around the downs. In the dark and the rain the small residual party of James, Paul, Fergus the dog and I set off in the gathering darkness and rain to walk the second six miles. This took just a gnat's tadger under two hours at about the pace we would like to achieve on the Challenge itself. I reckoned we were walking on reasonably similar underfoot conditions and with similar amounts of up-and-down. Very wet and stony in places, made a bit trickier due to it being dark.

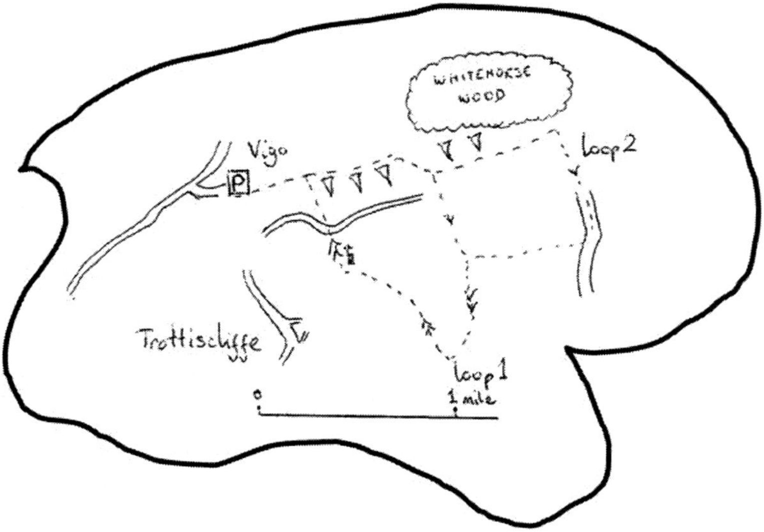

I actually like walking in the dark; navigation has to be more precise, the pay back is the landscape takes on a very different look and feel and you have a greater sense of remoteness and isolation than during daylight hours. Even walking around the Downs, which in reality is in close proximity to large urban areas and very close to at least two motorways, has the feel of being right out in the middle of nowhere during darkness hours.

Illumination can be a bit tricky. Mostly you walk on feel, placing your foot down and subconsciously testing the grip before your full weight is planted. Most head torches are worse than useless anyway. Unless you are prepared to carry around a car battery to power a lamp borrowed from the floodlights at the Sydney Cricket Ground you are left with a head torch that is useful for only two things;

1. Map reading
2. Blinding your fellow walkers when you turn around to talk to them

That being said it was a clear starry night wandering around Kent and we were even rewarded with the hooting of an owl accompanying us for half an hour or so.

By the end Paul looked shattered. By the time we drove to the pub he looked positively at deaths door, literally not figuratively. In fact if I didn't see him pick up his pint and drink it with my own eyes I would have sworn he had been exhumed especially for the purpose of sitting in the pub and looking terrible. The cold, clammy, congealed sweaty look is not yet fashionable, if it ever becomes so Paul can pull it off to a tee. Fergus wasn't much happier as the faithful hound was abandoned in the car as we went into the pub.

I constituted the walk as a fairly gentle 10 miles; the CC would be 54 miles of brisker pace and overall harder terrain. I reckoned at this point that Paul had two hopes of completing it - "Bob" and "Cape of Good". When I phoned him from home to check on his take away curry requirements (which I was ordering and we are all meeting to eat at my house) I was politely informed he couldn't make it as it was too far to walk. I've measured the distance; it is 383m from Paul's house to my house.

The aforementioned two hopes had been joined by their long lost brother "no". Eventually after a bath and some gentle persuasion he did join us for curry, and after eating his own body weight in naan bread (a speciality for both Paul and me) and a couple of reviving glasses of red wine he seemed a lot brighter. After the second after dinner malt he was positively optimistic again and we had a long debate about whether he could effectively train for a 54 mile walk by swimming a lot. Condensing the argument, I mean debate, down to the essential elements, the gist of it was he thought he could train in the pool and I didn't. My opinion was firmly in the walk/run/step/machine/cross trainer mode of training and when you get bored of all that do some more walking. This debate was a recurring theme; we had already had a similar debate in The Windmill after the October meet. It was difficult however to measure the effectiveness of Paul's swimming regime, as since October he hadn't put any of it into practice yet! Still the good point was he finished the walk and it now was beginning to get through to him what might be involved in this undertaking. His email from the following Monday confirmed that the message did seem to be getting through.........

From: [mailto:paul.martin]
Sent: 28 November 2005 09:46
To: John Milner
Cc: Iain Jackson; James Pilcher; Tony Kennedy
Subject: Re: How did you get on?

If you can imagine the Blair Witch Project intertwined with a Famous Five adventure (or three in our case but Jacko and myself could probably count for 2 each) you might be able to start visualizing the evening. On the whole it was a good litmus test for myself and the 54 mile jaunt has certainly got my attention as I was absolutely shagged after the 16.7km's.

Iain lead James and I straight as an arrow to each waypoint and at times we felt like debris being drawn in a comets wake, I also suspect there must be a bit of homing pigeon in him, because if it was down to me we would still be bumbling around the weald somewhere - so much appreciation and respect to Iain.

Good first stint - feeling a little afraid now.

Paul Martin
Charles Taylor Consulting

Paul's view was a little different to mine and yes we had our work cut out, but we did have time. Given enough effort in the next six months all of us could get in shape to do it. For sure it would test our commitment and effort as we built up the miles, but clearly build up the miles we had to.

The More Serious Work begins

Since we were all pretty much doing exactly what we had done before we couldn't really constitute ourselves as "in training" even though mentally we were definitely engaged. You can tell how connected we were with the CC because every time one or two of us got together we talked about it a lot. Uhm.... the time for procrastination was just about at an end and it was time we planned something that might at least constitute the start of proper training.

Christmas week was to be our first more serious effort. Most people were on holiday and by the end of Christmas week would probably have had their fill of food and drink. So Friday the 30th December became D-Day and a walk was planned of about 16 miles starting from home (Gravesend) walking out along the Thames and back along the Medway estuaries following the "Saxon Shore Way" to finally arrive in the village of Upnor.

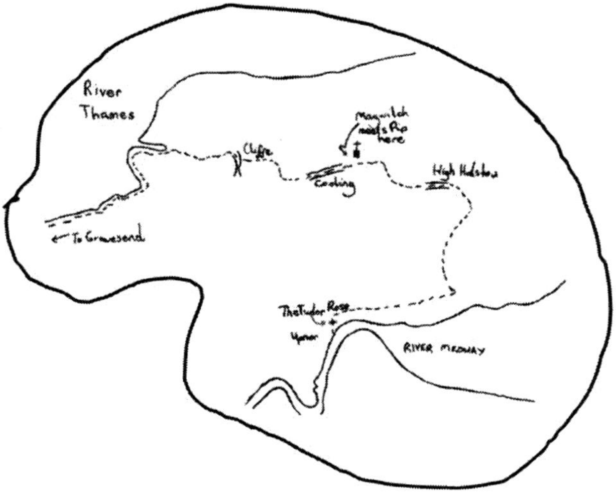

Metcheck, my favourite on line weather site, was not optimistic about our prospects, forecasting for days in advance a mixture of snow, sleet and rain. Since the plan was for the main party to rendezvous with the rest of the family at Northward Hill nature reserve and complete the last six miles together then the weather really could prove to be a huge stumbling block. It would be bad enough for us, but for the small people in the proposed family party it would definitely be a no-no in the forecast conditions.
I got up at 6:20; normally I'm a 6:55 alarm call for a 6:57 departure but with a long walk in front of me I wanted enough time for coffee, toast and most importantly a short spell in the smallest room.
I let the dogs out; starry sky, a bit cold but not too bad. Let the dogs back in five minutes later; snowing……….**a lot**. It could have been worse I suppose (I'm not sure how?) and armed with as many clothes as I could reasonably wear, a rucksack full of left over Xmas munchies and a large flask of sugary whisky laced coffee I set off together with Fergus. I even put a coat on Fergus (which I never do as I hate dogs dressed up), it was Baltic cold. Tosca, our small and fluffy Tibetan terrier, usually barks furiously if I take Fergus for a run and leave her behind. On this occasion she took one more look at the weather and trotted back off to bed in respectful silence. You could almost see her thinking about the insanity of the whole venture.
We duly met outside James's house at 7am and set off in the snowy darkness. By the time we walked through town and down to the river it was the half light just before dawn. It was a strange but rather beautiful landscape.
The light had a distinctly yellowish feel possibly from the snow or all the artificial light pollution. It's an odd

landscape, heavily industrialised with views to docks and power stations. In contrast out over the marshes the landscape is stark and remote and especially in the snow reminiscent of one of the atmospheric patches of a Dickens novel. The walk would indeed take us through one of Dickens's most used landscapes, especially in Great Expectations, more of that later. We stopped for a group portrait and a couple of snaps of the river and set off.

This time we were six. James, Paul, John, Mark, Fergus and me. Missing were Tony (holidaying in a Dutch Centerparcs) and David (still poorly). Third hand information seemed to imply David had already chucked in the towel and was migrating towards the role of driver, but in the end he didn't travel to Scotland at all.

Progress was pretty good especially considering the weather which was truly awful, snowing pretty heavily and bloody cold. At least the frozen ground provided fairly good underfoot conditions. The other positive factor was that the walk being mostly by the side of the estuary was more or less flat. It was easier going than anything undulating and importantly an even effort so you didn't have the phaff of exchanging layers of clothing for uphill

and ridge stretches as you do in the mountains. There was a simple mantra for today - put on all the clothes you have with you and don't take any off again.
I hate phaffing about it stretches my patience and I really didn't want to stand around on a day like this. Unfortunately I could see potential for an element of phaff in several of the team. John in particular had threatened to prove a world champion phaffer by seeming to take 10 minutes to put his boots on at the start having driven the 412m from his house to James's house as he was late.
I struggled a bit to be honest. By Cliffe Fort my legs went really heavy, about the same as they would after a five or six mile run and we had only walked about 8km. I put it down to an excess of Christmas goodies and too much sitting around. I put my head down, kept walking and said nothing. I wasn't going to admit any kind of difficulty in a hurry that would be too much like an admission of defeat. Fergus by contrast was flying. He loves being off his lead and as usual had assumed his self appointed role of group shepherd. This apparently endlessly satisfying pastime consists of running to the front of the group to check that all is well, and then running to the back (usually me) to make sure no one is lost. This might be a not too bad idea when walking 5 miles but I was pretty sure it was going to be a very bad idea when Fergus's previous high point was 11 miles and this was scheduled for a very cold wet 17 miles.
Reluctantly I put him on a lead, 500 yards later I remembered why this was such a bad idea. Fergus has another endearing habit. Hold the lead in your left hand and he walks on the right. Move it to the right and he switches to the left. Apart from the obvious answer of "nothing much" I struggle to figure out what happens inside my

dog's head. Anyway 500 yards of tripping over Fergus and swapping the lead from hand to hand was enough, I gave him a very stern lecture on the need to conserve energy and let him off again. He looked up saw two shadowy figures slightly ahead of us and ran off to check if it was indeed Paul and Mark and if they were OK. Since we were the only living souls within miles and they seemed to be walking in a more or less straight line I concluded the answer to both questions was probably yes. I gave up trying to educate Fergus and left him to his own devices. If he wanted to blow all his energy running backwards and forwards like a loon it was fine by me.

In reality there wasn't much to see on this bit of the walk. There is only so much pleasure you can derive from drinking in the landscape of West Tilbury power station and Canvey island oil refineries especially as any time you looked up a hail stone had a habit of hitting you directly on the eye ball which doesn't half sting.

Disappointingly in retrospect the route turns inland at Cliffe and you don't go out over Cliffe and Cooling marshes. You get a great view of these from the top of Northward Hill and these natural wetlands remain one of the few remaining natural marshes in the UK. It was a very wild landscape that day and it would have been interesting to continue on a more costal route to walk through the marshes.

It is over this small corner of unspoilt wildness, the only wild area in an otherwise homogeneously man made landscape, that some pillock in Westminster suggested building a new airport. How many bloody airports do we need? By the time we get them built aviation fuel will have started to go up in price dramatically as we finally wake up to the fact that oil reserves are not infinite. Air travel will become again the preserve of the rich and famous. In any

case call me cynical (and many do) but I am convinced this was never a real option. I reckon the government put it out as an obviously bad and stupid idea in order to make a new runway at Heathrow seem like not such a bad idea after all. Governments couldn't possibly do that could they?
Walking through Cliffe and Cooling villages is mostly on the road but it does offer an interesting diversion past the church yard featured in Great Expectations. Located here is an array of stone lozenges marking the gravestones of children, thirteen identical markers, ten all from one family. Dickens describes the location far better than I (he reduces the headstones to five) and on a day like today I am pretty sure it didn't feel so different from the time of his writing.

To five little stone lozenges, each about a foot and a half long, which were arranged in a neat row beside their grave, and were sacred to the memory of five little brothers of mine – who gave up trying to get a living, exceedingly early in that universal struggle – I am indebted for a belief I religiously entertained that they had all been born on their backs with their hands in their trouser-pockets, and had never taken them out in this state of existence.
Ours was the marsh country, down by the river, within, as the river wound, twenty miles of the sea. My first most vivid impression of the identity of things, seems to me to have been gained on a memorable raw afternoon towards evening. At such time I found out for certain, that this bleak place overgrown with nettles was the churchyard; and that Philip Pirrip, late of this parish, and also Georgiana wife of the above, were dead and buried; and that Alexander, Bartholomew, Abraham, Tobias, and Roger, infant children of the aforesaid, were also dead and buried; and that the dark flat wilderness beyond the churchyard, intersected with dykes and mounds and gates, with scattered cattle feeding on it, was the marshes; and that the low leaden line beyond , was the river; and that the distant savage lair from which the wind was rushing, was the sea; and that the small bundle of sensations growing afraid of it all and beginning to cry, was Pip.

I'd like to say we stopped and contemplated how much tougher life was in Dicken's time, but we didn't. It was too bloody cold. If we had stopped there I think I might have felt like Pip and cried. We marched straight past with barely an acknowledged grunt to me imparting my bit of Dicken's trivia and stopped instead outside the public toilets just down the road. At least the public toilets had a sort of overhang from the roof we could kind of huddle under and get out of the weather. Exchanging a hundred or so years of history for a dry spot was a fair trade in the circumstances. It had stopped snowing by then and started sleeting instead. Nice.

We fuelled up on a mixture of left over Xmas cake, jelly babies and a large malt. Smart arses who want to tell me that alcohol dilates the capillaries and increases heat loss can be assured I already know that but was quite prepared to take the risk when we were twenty yards from civilisation. If I was walking in the Scottish mountains in winter it would be a different prospect, but on the Saxon Shore Way I felt I could risk it.

In any case the one of us who was really cold was Fergus. Despite the best efforts of his coat he was shivering badly and refused the proffered dog chews. Luckily John had partially filled his lunchbox with leftover turkey and this proved much more to Fergus's liking. He stopped shivering for long enough to scoff the lot.

The only other job for the stop was to phone the other half's at home and see if they were indeed going to meet us for the last six miles. Put succinctly I think the message was "no fear". We agreed to meet in Upnor as they were going to take a saunter along the beach and that was our intended finishing route. Failing that we would meet in the pub, naturally.

At this point, a bit over half way, everyone was still going well. Paul was certainly in better shape than at the end of the ten miler. John and James were in fine fettle. Mark,

saying very little, smoking an occasional roll up, and incredibly wearing soaking wet jeans, looked like if we put a brick wall in front of him he would walk straight through it. He creates an equal amount of admiration and annoyance in me. Admiration because he is clearly fit, and pretty tough, and annoyance because he seems to achieve it with precious little effort. Bastard.
I was about the same level of heavy leggedness as I had been at Shorne Fort and in fact stayed pretty much like that the whole day. Not on tip top form but least not getting increasingly weary as we progressed.
As we left the shelter afforded by the roof of the public toilets the snow relented and gave way instead to an unpleasant sleet. The route, still following the Saxon Shore Way, now took us round to the North of Northward Hill and then up to the top of the hill through the RSPB nature reserve. This is the high point of the whole Hoo peninsula and the only minor bit of uphill walking for the day. From the top of the hill the view over the marshes extends over the Thames Estuary to Southend. The estuary looked to be an inhospitable place today. The sea had a deep coffee colour about the colour of a bad cup of machine instant without enough powdered milk in it.

The occasional white horse confirmed it was pretty windy out there and although it was a bit unpleasant where we were I knew it was a lot worse out at sea. It reminded me of the one occasion I was nearly sea sick. I used to own a half share in a Folkboat. These are really a thing of great beauty, no plastic pig here. 29 feet long and built of mahogany planks on oak timbers with a fixed lead keel. Ours, named Persuasion, had been built in Poland in the early 1960's and weighed in at nearly six tons. The construction had its downside in that it took six coats of yacht varnish a year to keep her seaworthy but compensations in the admiring glances from everyone when you arrived in a marina. Her great ability was to sit comfortably in a big sea. With such a heavy and robust construction and a relatively narrow beam she sat low in the water and ploughed through any reasonable sea. Some of my friends glass fibre alternatives float on top of the water like a gigantic ping pong ball and you were tossed hither and thither in a big sea.

The one occasion that was brought to mind by today's conditions was one of those days that started with a one hour debate on the wisdom of venturing out. We were moored in Queenborough, tucked in the River Swale just off the Isle of Sheppey at the confluence of the Thames and the Medway. The wind was from the NE and as such we were at least partly sheltered from the wind and since our planned trip was across the estuary to Bradwell we knew it would be a very tough ride beating against the wind most of the way. After much deliberation we eventually set off and had not even reached the end of the Swale when we knew it was getting difficult. My mate, who was far more experienced than me, and also passed for what "*Perception*" could constitute as a skipper, was trying to read the chart whilst I tried to sail and identify the names on the passing buoys. Sailing was a bit of a misnomer really it consisted of crashing into a wave, the foredeck disappearing and the boat would stop. The main-sail flapped for a bit then filled again and the boat picked up until it flew off the next wave to bury the foredeck again and the process would repeat. It wasn't really that bad, I guess it was blowing a five maybe gusting six but it does give me total respect for Ocean going yachts men and women who sail in enormous seas in the Southern Ocean.

My trouble started when the skipper cried foul on navigating, surfaced up top and sent me down below to read the chart. The chart table was in a really bad spot on our boat. It wasn't gimballed so in this sea it sat at a very jaunty angle and to boot it was located directly above the engine. This left you with one foot on a bunk, one foot on the floor trying to focus on a chart whilst the boat crashed up and down and you breathed in a healthy aroma of bilge water and petrol fumes. I can honestly say it is the only time on board a boat I've felt a bit queasy. We abandoned the venture and headed back to Queenborough. That was even worse as the boat surfed down the waves and occasionally a wave would overtake you break and swamp the cockpit. I was a bit scared to be honest.
As I said this was tame stuff by ocean going standards but quite enough for me and looking out to the estuary today I was glad to be on dry land. Strangely I couldn't see any white sails battling up the river on this day in December.

As you leave the woods at Northward Hill, our route along the Saxon Shore Way turned to cut across the Hoo Peninsula and head due South. The wind, a bitter South Easterly, cut through us badly. We were heartily glad we didn't have any small people with us. A cold wind has a draining effect on you like almost no other weather. It is like someone pulled a plug out of the bottom of your foot and let your energy and warmth drain away. At 44 years and 19 stone this happens fairly slowly if you are eight years old and weigh five stone you can grind to a halt pretty quickly.

Fergus (six years old three stone) hadn't ground to a halt but he had given up his previous herding nature and was walking fairly glumly by my side. He had had enough. It was pissing down by now. The temperature had gone up one or two degrees since we departed but it was more than compensated for by wind and rain. We were collectively in mono syllabic trudge mode. Nobody's mood improved when I made a navigation error and added a totally unnecessary two miles to the route. By this stage it was a case of getting it done. Mark and James were striding ahead; I couldn't keep up with them. Paul was at the back muttering and struggling along, this did not constitute pleasure. We were heading parallel to the Medway towards Upnor which is a very old historic village with a proud naval history. Sitting on the shore of the Medway it lays directly opposite Chatham dockyard a home for building naval vessels since the 16th century.

The narrowness of the Medway at this point made Chatham reach a defendable anchorage for the British fleet and to mind this rather valuable asset Henry VIII commissioned and built Upnor castle in 1559.

The castle was only partially effective in its role as in 1667 the Dutch sailed bold as brass up the Medway and made off with the English flagship of the day. Although they took a substantial hammering from fire from Upnor and other gun placements this was none the less cocking a snoop at the English by stealing the pride of the fleet from what was deemed such a safe harbour.

I tend to believe that the Dutch must have picked a day after the local whisky club meet when the English manning the gun places were dozing off a rather large helping of local beverage as it is hard to see how they "sneaked" up the Medway otherwise and made off with the pride of the fleet.

For obvious reasons the best view of the castle is from the river where it stands proud over the seascape and commands some respect. From land side it is less impressive and is now run by English heritage. Of course it is also a sodding wedding venue, as it seems is every picturesque building in the South East of England over twenty years old.

Eventually the village of Upnor hove into view and the prospect of beer and butties improved the mood and the pace. We had long since abandoned any thoughts of meeting the girls on the beach at Upnor and made a bee line directly to the pub. The pub, The Tudor Rose, had done us proud and created a mountain of food perfect for refuelling, and to boot an excellent pint of Spitfire can be had here. John was under severe time stress so I had volunteered to drive him directly back to Gravesend. The 30 minute round trip had me return to the pub to see what clearly had once been a substantial spread of soup, sandwiches, roast spuds and chips looking not unlike it had been set upon by a flock of magpies. Paul was tucking into what it transpired was

his fourth bowl of chicken soup with a delicate crouton garnish consisting of a cheese doorstep sandwich and two roast spuds.
Luckily Alison had saved me some food and despite the bedraggled appearance of the buffet table there was quite a lot left so no shortage of carbs for me either,
Fergus was on about his fifth roast spud by then, and was not looking happy. In particular he looked very pissed off if I went near him and when we went to leave the pub steadfastly refused to come with me. It was Alison holding his lead or nothing clearly Dad was far too dangerous when it came to walkies!

Paul, as usual provided a very neat summary of where we were on the path to being fully prepared for 54 miles, with his email summary of the post walk pain content.

```
Iain,

Knee was a bit puffy for a day or so (but it
could have been soup overflow), it certainly hurt
towards the end but I am encouraged by the fact
that it did not stop working. Next walk will be
aided by as many drugs as I can manage before
liver damage becomes a worry.

Thanks for the 30th it was excellently planned
executed, we certainly are a disparate bunch and
need determined glue like you to foster team
spirit.
```

What is the expected distance of the next walk so I can start to gauge the quantity of Vaseline and the elasticity of underwear needed.

Regards

Paul Martin
Charles Taylor Consulting

19.2 miles was the final verdict and only 197m of climbing The Caledonian Challenge would be 54 miles and over 2000m of climbing. We had a long, long way still to go but at least now we could actually say we had started.

The Gravesend Windmill Hill Scottish Malt Whisky Society

· ACT ONE : ..."THE ARRIVAL OF THE DUCK"... ·

ANDY P. : GOOD JOB MEL LOVES HOUSEWORK.
JAMES P. : I MUST MINUTE THAT.
PAUL M. : I COULD EAT A HORSE... BUT A DUCK WILL DO.
MARK D. : DO YOU KNOW I RAN 4 MILES IN 12½ MINUTES TODAY.
LAWRENCE A. : 9/10 FOR THIS ONE... LOVELY AND PEATY
STEWART D. : YES, BEST WHISKY I HAVE HAD IN THE LAST HOUR.
DAVID L. : I NEVER USED TO LIKE WHISKY.
JOHN M. : HAVE I TOLD YOU ABOUT MY NEW BAGS?
TONY K. : CAN'T WAIT FOR THE ARM WRESTLING.
IAIN J. : IF WE PLAY FORMULA 1, I WILL HAVE TO SHOOT MYSELF.

Some of you might feel that The Gravesend Windmill Hill Scottish Malt Whisky Society is a very long name for a bunch of old soaks who meet occasionally to get absolutely trolleyed on fine Scottish whisky. You would of course be absolutely correct; in fact our little collective barely merits the title of club or society at all.

The original idea for the whisky club had been from James. A long time lover of Scottish whisky he had for some time been milling around the idea of getting a group of likeminded fellows together to sample a few choice malts. Enlisting me was the simplest of tasks. As I mentioned earlier I am also a long time fan of every single whisky I've ever drunk (with the possible exception of Cutty Sark a rather severe blend that does actually need something mixed with it before it becomes palatable) and without actually having much idea what I was signing up for I immediately said yes to James's suggested whisky club. Paul was already another whisky lover who joined at the first hint of a plan. Tony says yes to everything since his pathological optimism leads him to conclude that everything is a good idea. Mark lived next door to James so despite claiming not to like whisky he also joined on the basis it wasn't far to walk.

Lawrence and David threw their hats in the ring and so on the 16th June 2003 the GWHSMWS was born.

Our initial ideas for the whisky club now look to be just a tad on the lofty side. The original email discussion was debating whether one bottle would be enough; Paul was bold enough to suggest we might need two bottles for a meeting.

Dear James,

What a fabulous idea but I have 2 q's
Do we have to limit ourselves to Malt Whisky, I am in favour and whole heatedly support the consumption of a wide variety of whisky – as you know to your cost.
I think maybe 1 bottle between 6 people may not be enough (this may be a case of my eye bigger than my belly no comments please),
So for each host there could be a co host that supplies another bottle just a thought.

Regards

Paul Martin
Charles Taylor Consulting

In the cold light of 2007 that looks a tiny bit optimistic. Our numbers have now swelled to eleven (membership has been closed at eleven although a recent resolution does allow the host to invite two guests per meeting) and our consumption runs at about four bottles a meeting. On average with three meets a year (more would result in liver failure) we have consumed in the four years since foundation a staggering forty three bottles of whisky. Here they are in the approximate chronological order of drinking:

Cadenhead Speyside (2 off), Edradour (2 off), Dalwhinnie (2 off), Lagavulin, Balvenie, Glengoyne, Long John (David brought that don't know how it got into a malt whisky club), Glenkinchie, Aberlour (2off), Talisker, Bruichladdich, Highland Park, Bowmore, Glenmacadam, Glenfiddich, Cambletown, Cadenhead Rosebank, Macallan,

Balvenie 15 year old special, Glenlivet, Fettercairn, Glen Garioch, Cadenhead Glenkinchie, Tobermory (2 off) Ardbeg, Tormore, Glenmorangie, Glenfiddich 15 year old, Cadenhead Glenroth, Balblair, Cadenhead Glenlivet, Glen Gassaugh, Jura, Old Pultney, and Ardbeg.

Fantastic.

Before the first meeting we were even drawing up rules. Heaven knows why since after one hour of each meeting it is total anarchy anyway. Still for the record here were our original rules.

THE WINDMILL HILL SCOTTISH MALT WHISKY SOCIETY RULES

Purpose
The purpose of the society is to pursue the appreciation and consumption of the finest Scottish whisky and to be true to that famous beverage as the "Water of Life".

Meetings

Meetings of the society are to be held at least once every three calendar months. It is responsibility of the host (see "host" below) to convene the meeting and agree a mutually agreeable date for the meeting.

Host for the inaugural meeting will be Mr. James Pilcher.

Responsibilities

Each member of the society will be appointed a responsibility which tenant he will hold for a single meeting. Responsibilities will be reapportioned for the next meeting by the host.

Host

The key part of the meeting, the host shall

- Fix a date for the meeting
- Supply one bottle of malt whisky for tasting and drinking the balance of which he shall retain at the end of the evening.
- Host or supply a venue for the meeting
- Assign remaining roles for the meeting

The host should apply great care in the choice of whisky considering previous tasting and giving equal weight to all of the fine whisky regions: Highland, Lowland, Speyside, Islay, Islands and giving particular merit to rare whisky or that from sadly now closed distilleries.

Cook

Cook shall supply ample food for the evening. Choice of food should ideally reflect Scotland's cuisine but should not require elaborate or excessive preparation and should be incidental to the general proceedings of the evening.

Beer Monitor

In Scotland there is an old and wise saying

If you drink whisky alone your drunk before you're full.
If you drink beer alone your full before you're drunk.
If you drink beer and whisky together you're drunk and full at the same time.

While the WHSMWS is not pursuing either fullness or drunkenness a certain amount of beer can be complementary to the enjoyment of some whisky and the beer monitor has the responsibility to provide such beverage.

Games Master

Games master provides a certain level of entertainment for the evening for example an appointed board or card game. The game should be known by all or trivially easy to learn and should be complete in time for quiet reflection and conversation for the latter part of the evening.

All

Although the host has specific whisky duties other members of the society should feel free to bring a particular favourite along for sampling by one or more of the members.

Now if you want the full picture on the utter futility and irrelevance of rules I can paint it very simply. James faithfully keeps minutes from every single meeting (good chap that he is) here is a sample extracted from the start of meeting number one:

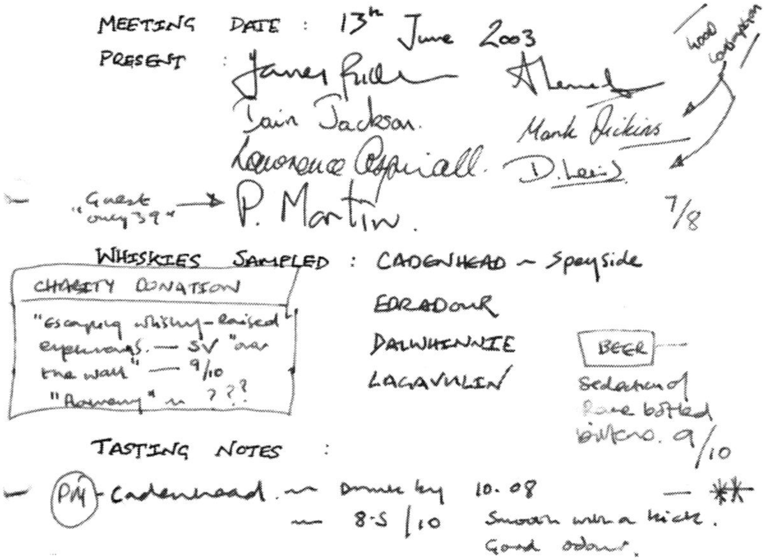
MEETING DATE : 13th June 2003

PRESENT : James Fuller

Iain Jackson. Mark Dickins

Lawrence D. Lewis

"Guest only 39" → P. Martin. 7/8

WHISKIES SAMPLED : CADENHEAD ~ Speyside

EDRADOUR

DALWHINNIE

LAGAVULIN

CHARITY DONATION

"Escaping whisky-raised experiences. — SV "over the wall" — 9/10

"Anyway" ~ ???

BEER — Selection of rare bottled bitters. 9/10

TASTING NOTES :

PM - Cadenhead ~ drunk by 10.08 — **

~ 8.5/10 Smooth with a kick. Good odour.

And here is a sample from the minutes of meeting number five written sometime around 11:23 pm:

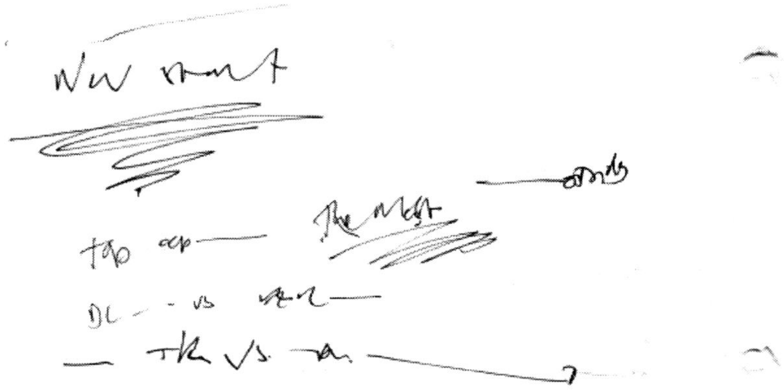

The more perceptive amongst you will have detected noticeable differences in the calligraphy between the two sets of minutes. Putting it simply, whilst scribing the second set of minutes James was completely, well for want of a better word, bollocksed.

If your chairman can't speak or stay awake, rules seem a little bit of overkill. Now I don't want to create the wrong impression here as it is never our intention at the outset of a whisky club meet to over indulge it is just sort of hard not to. As I alluded to earlier whisky drinking is a kind of a self fulfilling prophecy, the more you drink the better it tastes and the more you want to drink right up to the point where you have to go home and speak to the wife. This particular task has the inevitable and entirely understandable conclusion of a night spent sleeping it off in the spare room.

We do actually try to have some kind of competitive elements to most whisky nights. Events have so far included conkers, scaletrix, pub games, pitch and put (before drinking not during), impromptu arm wrestling (subsequently banned as too dangerous), and Formula One.

Formula One I discovered is an ancient and intensely irritating board game that James has preserved since the age of twelve. I say it belongs in the Antiques Road Show and steadfastly refuse to play it ever again as it is simply ridiculous. My opinion has nothing at all to do with the fact that when I was clearly winning hands down a lucky throw of the dice by Milner blocked me at the last corner and I had to observe all and sundry stream past me. Nothing what so ever.

Andy Parr invented and conclusively won hands down one of the better whisky club contests. Called simply "How do I ruin the kitchen so that my wife won't speak to me for at least a week after the whisky club" his undeniably spectacular victory was achieved by spinning round at high speed to talk to someone whilst holding a tray of very hot confit of duck. The resulting tidal wave of duck fat that escaped from the roasting tray and redistributed itself over five square yards of kitchen was bad enough. His attempts to repair the damage by mopping said duck fat with an old tea towel had the dubious benefit of spreading hot duck fat over every square inch of kitchen that had escaped the first tidal wave. A world class performance. In ten minutes of endeavour he created a scene straight out of the worst bits of How Clean Is Your House. We all agreed Mel would be extremely considerate and since Andy would have a horrible hang over she would be only too pleased to spend Saturday morning trying to clean congealed duck fat from every corner of her rather lovely kitchen. Or perhaps not.....

Andy bless him is also joint owner of an equally valued trophy. Not the annual conker, golf or pub games trophies (no surprise Mark has won all three for the last twenty seven years in a row) he holds the prize for "How to destroy large parts of your friends house" competition in partnership with my good self.

The annual conker championship has been "livened up" by the ancient Scottish practice of "stampsies". This was all the rage in our play ground when I was at primary school. If you drop your conker, or if the string breaks you'd better recover it quickly because whilst on the ground the conker is fair game for a bit of rough treatment with a size twelve boot. The really practiced in the art, like me, aim not for the opposition conker but for their string. This results in good old tangle a strong tug usually finds one or both conkers on the floor. A swift stamp with the boot on the opposition conker and it is game over. Of course as the opposition get wise to this tactic they take precautionary measures, like extended string wrapped multiple times round the fingers. On the rare occasion the string breaks and the conker hits the deck they also react quickly and a certain amount of pushing and shoving ensues.

It was this solution to a Parr vs. Jackson conker match that took conkers closer to the realms of the WWF (world wrestling federation although world wildlife fund would also do) than the boy scouts. Parr and Jackson began wrestling for conker supremacy outside Milner's front door to end prostrate in his kitchen having removed several pieces of his house along the way. We were not really flavour of the month chez Milner after that display and stampsies were banned, at least for a while.

Lists are also a favourite whisky club past time, you will have detected already my own passion for listing things. Amongst lists created have been, Leeds United team of the 1970's, 11 most boring cricketers ever to play test cricket (you can guess what this looked like. Let's just say there was a heck of a lot of Boycott on the team sheet only interrupted to make way for Trevor Bailey batting at number seven) and my own personal favourite "Women you fancy but shouldn't". The rather curious collection of apparently fanciable females went as follows:

Anna Ford, Glenda Jackson, Delia Smith, Sue Barker, Virginia Wade, Edwina Curry, Val Singleton, Carol Vorderman, Margot from the Good Life, Anneka Rice, The Queen, Suzi Quatro, Felicity Kendall, Babs in Pans People, Gladys Emmanuel, Kirsty Alsop, Joanna Lumley, Helen Mirren, Joan Collins and Cheri Blair.

At the meeting after this list was generated a review of previous minutes resulted in a serious witch hunt to find the culprit(s) who fronted up with The Queen and Cheri Blair but no one owned up. As someone might say there were only seven people who could answer that question. The six people still awake when the list had been generated and God. The whisky club membership had severe whisky induced amnesia and God wasn't forthcoming with an answer. Given the rest of the list it is perhaps a little surprising God did not make the list himself, or at the very least a female representative such as Mary Magdeline or Thora Hird.

The very best moments at whisky club meets are simply though the quiet contemplation of the finer things in life with your mates. Sitting on a summer evening in the garden with a glass of reasonably expensive whisky and a few mates does lead to the pondering of just how exceedingly lucky we all are. OK so we might think we work hard and modern working life does have its stresses not least the time commitment needed to hold down a job, but its neither physically demanding nor dangerous in the way coal mining or fishing were for our grandparents. In almost every other aspect of our lives we are extremely privileged. We choose what to eat and drink, we have really solid families and mates, and in the quieter moments at a whisky club you feel the warmth of friendship as something solid and valuable in life.

I usually respond to these quiet contemplations round about 11:45 by falling asleep.

A Darwinian self preservation mechanism has been built into my constitution such that just before I consume the fatal extra whisky that will result in an absolutely crippling hang over my body shuts down and I'm asleep. Even in mid sentence I can drop off in a sleep that can only be disturbed by nuclear attack or by it being time to go home. James usually records this faithfully in the minutes and in every set can be found a few words on Jackson slumbering.

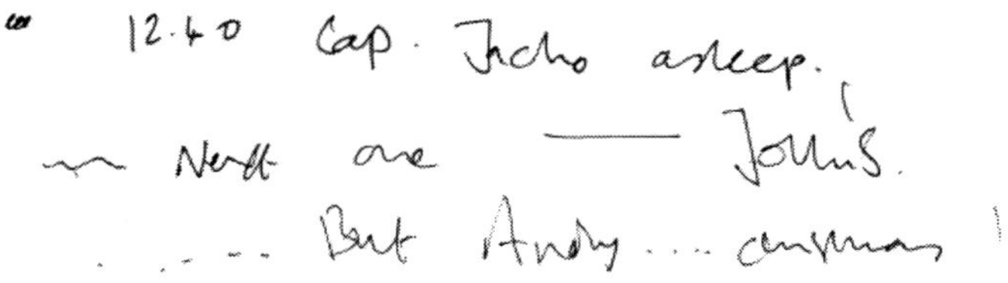

The discerning of you will also see that James late night calligraphy has improved since meeting five. A careful next day review of the meeting five minutes led him to the conclusion that in the interest of posterity he ought to preserve at least enough sobriety to record the end of each meeting. Either that or Christine told him if he came back from whisky club meetings in the same state as he reached in meeting five it was two choices:

1. Divorce
2. Resign from the whisky club

Whatever his motivation he has remained true to his promise and subsequent meetings have (mostly) legible minutes.

Of course the real point of whisky club evening is rather self evidently whisky. This most remarkable of beverages has been the subject of endless scribing from scholars and authors far more erudite than I. The whisky club tasting notes mostly take the form of scores out of 10 and one line comments. A few random descriptions give you the sense of our abilities as connoisseurs:

"good odour" Cadenhead Glenlivet
"session whisky" Edradour
"nice – spicy – not going to rip your balls of" Glen Goyne 17 years
"piece of piss" Dalwhinie
"Paint stripper" Lagavulin
"One of the best, superb, light and fruity," Cadenhead Rosebank

The not so discerning whisky club membership though still seem capable of draining to the last drop whisky labelled paint stripper or piece of piss. There has not been a single meeting where any of the whisky has been left, apart of course from the occasion David brought Long John along. I think some of the fascination stems from the beautiful simplicity of the thing. Most of the Scottish distilleries offer tours and in each the process is basically the same. To make malt whisky you do the following: germinate some barley then dry it in peat smoke; mix with hot water, drain and add yeast; ferment; drain and distil the liquid throwing away the first bit of the distillation and the last bit (I think they call it the head and the tail but I could be wrong and if you want to be really picky I think they recycle one or both of them). Anyway keep the bit from the middle of the distillation and put into a wooden barrel, French oak for example. Leave for ten or more years. Bottle. Simple and from that one basic process you get an enormous range of tastes, odours and strengths. Three ingredients barley, yeast and water, six simple processes, malting, drying, mashing, fermenting, distilling, maturing and you have your product. Magnificent.

If reincarnation does exist I will return as *Torula Compniacensis Richon*. About 2 % of the whisky stored in barrels is lost every year to evaporation the distillers call it the angels share. Actually a lot of it never reaches the angels because the very smart black fungus *Torula Compniacensis Richon* thrives on alcoholic vapours. If you visit a distillery or even drive past one don't mistake the black appearance of the buildings as soot is actually a liberal coating of the happiest fungus in the world.

So there you have it whisky the water of life. If you claim not to like it at least go and try a really nice malt. You don't have to go mad get a bottle of Maderia wood finished Glenmorangie, add a little soft water and sip. If you still claim to not like whisky then stop reading here and give this book to a friend who might actually appreciate the better things in life.

• ACT TWO : ... "LATER THAT EVENING" ... •

ANDY P : MEL WILL KILL ME ..

PAUL M : I'M STILL HUNGRY .. ANYTHING ELSE TO EAT ?

JAMES P : ....

MARK D : THIS IS THE BEST EXERCISE I HAVE HAD ALL DAY.

STEWART O : SO, WOMEN YOU FANCY BUT SHOULDN'T.

DAVID L : MARGARET THATCHER ?

JOHN M : ANGELA RIPPON ?

TONY R : PLEASE CAN WE DO SOME ARM WRESTLING ?

IAIN J : ..ZZZZ....

A proper walk.

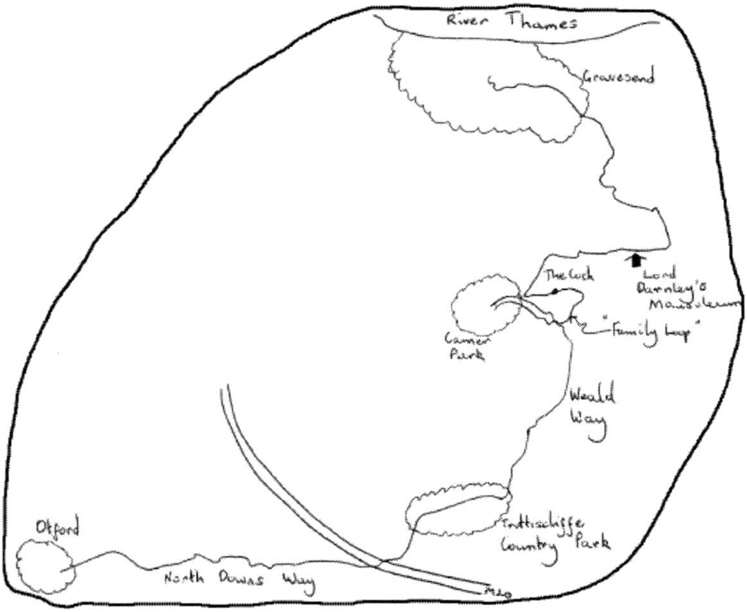

The Xmas walk was a good challenge. The crappy weather increased the degree of difficulty several notches and gave everyone a fitness and gear wake up call. Several of our team had gone out and bought new boots and coats, some of them had even worn them! Paul, who it has to be said, was the main concern to be fully prepared in time, was now getting off the train at Cannon Street and walking to the Strand. A small increase in distance, but done every day it had to help. In preparing for a 54 mile walk you simply cannot do enough walking. In an ideal world 10 miles a day with a 25 mile walk every weekend would be the training program of choice. Of course that's not going to happen as there are too many other choices to be made prioritising work and family above completing the Caledonia Challenge. Most of us are equally unlikely to give up all forms of drink and bad food and follow Dr Gillian Mckeith's "you are what you eat" plan to get down to 15% body fat and a state of optimal hydration. For us balance was more about doing whatever exercise could be fitted in and re-hydrating thoroughly after our long walks with six pints of Stella.

So the next walk loomed. The target this time was 27 miles with substantially more up and down than the flat walk along the river. An invite was duly distributed:

From: Jackson, Iain
Sent: 23 January 2006 11:35
To: 'Tony.Kennedy@blueyonder.co.uk'; 'john.milner@BailyGarner.co.uk'; 'Paul.martin@ctcplc.com'; 'james Pilcher (jpilcher@caxtons.com)'; 'andy.parr@mindshareworld.com'; 'jackson@shrubberyroad.freeserve.co.uk'
Cc: Jackson, Iain; 'stewart.owen@hotmail.com'
Subject:

Next training walk is Sunday the 5th Feb. Rough agenda
Meet outside James's house at 6:20 am for a 6:30 departure.
Drive to Otford start walking at around 7 am
1st leg to Camer park is 14 miles, meet any families who want to join us for a bit at Camer park at about 12:30
Do a roughly 3-4 mile loop with dogs and families if the weather is nice enough stop at The Cock or Golden Lion for a drink. I suggest we don't plan lunch at the pub because if the weather is not good we probably won't want to hang around and if the

weather is good there will be loads of us and it will take ages to get any food. So bring your own sandwiches is the best bet.
Depart families after that and walk back to Gravesend via Cobham, The Mausoleum and Shorne Country Park a further 9 miles.
Can you let me know if you plan to be there we hopefully can all fit in one car to get out to Otford.
I expect we would finish back at Gravesend around 5:30pm. I know it is a bit of a long day but should be really quality training.
The attached map shows the route.
Cheers
Iain

The route would take us from Otford along the North Downs Way to Trottiscliffe Country Park. From there we would head north along the Weald Way to rendezvous with families at Camer Park. A short loop of 4 miles with the family, including of course a compulsory stop in The Cock at Luddesdowne, would leave us with 9 miles to walk back to Gravesend via Lord Darnley's mausoleum and Shorne Country Park.
This time we were quorate; John, James, Tony, Mark, Paul, Fergus and my good self were the walking team for the day to be joined for the lunch time family loop by a further three dogs, six adults and seven children.

We for once collected in good time and at 6:30 am sharp departed in James's people carrier to Otford. I had a new strategy planned for Fergus this time, given how totally shagged out he was after the 20 mile Xmas jaunt. This time I was going to keep him on his lead and conserve his strength. I figured that if he played the walking under my feet game too much then by the time I had accidentally

landed my size twelve's on his paws a couple of times he would get the hang of it and keep to one side or the other, at least that was the theory. Parking up in Otford station we piled out of the car eager to get going and then stood around for the obligatory ten minutes while John phaffed around. Having half emptied his rucksack it transpired that every individual item was neatly packed in its own small canvas bag. One for the camera, one for the GPS, one the penknife, I'd swear even the water bottle had its own mini rucksack to live in. With no discernible change in the contents John re-packed his rucksack, found a blister plaster for Mark, who had gouged half of his foot away with a new pair of shin pads playing footie the previous day, and finally we could get going.

As you leave Otford the first part of the North Downs Way takes you up to the top of Otford Mount which is a steady but not unpleasant pull. The day promised much, the weather was the very best of winter weather, clear skies with a slight chill, one of those mornings when you can taste the freshness of the air. Paul chugged ahead at a speed

he and everyone else knew he couldn't keep up, but he can't stop himself! A quarter of an hour sees you to the top of the hill and a view over the Weald of Kent and the village of Kemsing. At least we thought it was probably Kemsing. Our almost limitless capacity for talking absolute rubbish whilst walking along surfaced in spades as a thirty minute debate ensued about whether the village that had hove into view was Kemsing or not. One day I'll have to go to Kemsing, judging from the amount of mental energy and focus it spawned it really must be something special.

From here the Weald of Kent really does look like the garden of England. Even in early February it looks green and pleasant, a large fertile plain divided into the patchwork quilt of fields so stereotypically representative of English countryside. Ambling through this landscape on a cold (but not bitterly so) morning was really very pleasant and the first 6 and a bit miles passed very pleasantly taking in the view and chatting amiably about nothing very much.
After six miles we arrived near Trosley Country Park at the foot of the escarpment for the North Downs. A fairly steady

pull up brought us to the café in Trosley Country Park and the most essential of beverages hot tea. At this stage everyone felt pretty well satisfied with a couple of times up and down the downs and six steady miles. Paul and Tony being group optimists had extrapolated the ease of completing six miles to the entire 54 miles endeavour and were now “pretty confident” about the whole enterprise. Tony can remain optimistic in the face of incontrovertible evidence to the contrary. Paul by contrast starts to sag visibly as his feet hurt and his stomach rumbles. A quick analysis of optimism amongst our team profiles the day quite nicely, being a geeky engineering type at heart it really needs a graph to properly describe it.

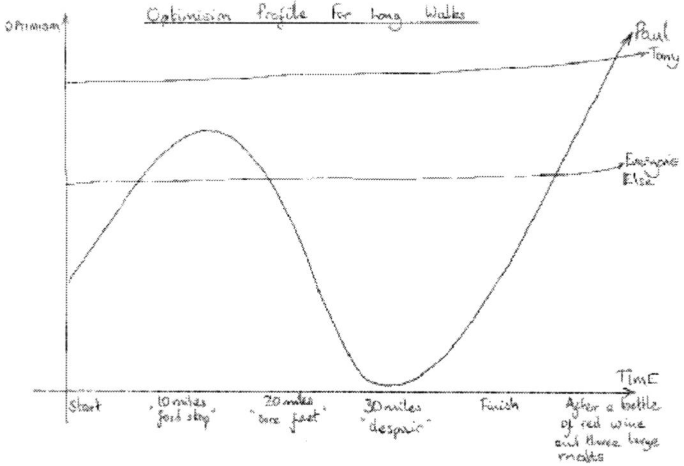

More cheery trudging commenced with another sortie to the foot of the downs at the end of Trosley Country Park where we joined the Weald Way and immediately ascended the Downs again to much general grumbling about the choice of route. I consoled everyone by promising that we had now completed the serious up and down (no pun intended) work for the day which was pretty true. As a microcosm of the real event it had some purpose as much of the ascent and descent involved in the Caledonian Challenge is compressed into the first twenty miles so it was good to get some serious hill work in followed by a long plod.

At this point we had barely passed anyone, the occasional dog walker in Trosley Country Park being the sum of our fellow early morning fresh air seekers. As we headed through the back of someone's farm yard and on towards Great Buckland we passed a man, a dog and a ferret. Since the man appeared to be carrying what looked exactly like a rifle and didn't look like he wanted to exchange pleasantries with a bunch of invading townies, we mumbled a silent good morning and carried on our way. One can only assume that the rabbit population of Great Buckland is held in check by the combination of early morning, man, dog, ferret and gun.

Moving on swiftly we crossed to the best part of the walk. The Weald Way gently ascends from Great Buckland running at a diagonal to the valley. Eventually as you crest the hill above Luddesdown a 180 degree turn gives a panorama of peaceful valley strewn with copses. OK so as Basil famously said you can't see herds of Wildebeest sweeping majestically across the plains, but for Kent, and only a few miles from the M25 it was still a view worth working for.

The weather decided to parallel our generally optimistic mood and as we walked up the valley towards our rendezvous with the rest of our families at Camer Park the sun broke through and adding to the good progress of the day we arrived at Camer Park exactly on schedule at 12:30.

Of course it can never be simple to rendezvous six walkers and a dog with a further five adults, seven children and three dogs and we were back into the herding cats exercise of how to get everyone in the same place at the same time. This was due in no small part to James having conveyed to Christine we were meeting at 1 pm and Christine having obligingly phoned all the other halves to let them know we were running half an hour late even though we were bang on time. Don't ask me how this happened, but all I can tell you is Paddy Power the bookmaker would give you no better than 4-6 on a cock up in the logistics and around 6-1 on things running smoothly with such a large and varied herd trying to convene at an appointed place and time. Anyway, rendezvous we eventually did and sauntered of as a large gang of 22 and wandered off via Luddesdowne to "The Cock" for lunch. It is hard to visit the Cock and not drink beer and despite all promises to be good we couldn't resist a small amount of re-hydration with a pint of foaming ale. Sitting in the sunshine with a few miles already tromped drinking a pint of proper beer is amongst life's finest pleasures and today was no exception. A pint of Adnams Southwold disappeared in approximately three minutes; I remain convinced to this day someone else drank most of mine.

What was considerably less fun was putting boots back on and setting off again knowing we had a further 9 miles to go, but after a brief twenty minutes or so we left the rest of the gang enjoying the sunshine and carried on our way. It would be safe to say that if anyone walking their dog had passed us over the next hour or so they might have doubted our sanity. At John's behest we started a game of "countries". Not too difficult. You start with the letter A and name in turn a country beginning with A and carry on in turn until all possibilities have been exhausted. Last person to name a country wins. Of course since we didn't have an Atlas with us and since some principalities insist on changing their name regularly there was a fair amount of dispute. Is British Honduras a country? Is Burma, Burma or Myanmar? How about the Balearics or Bahrain? And that was only on "B".

The standard of play also varied enormously from Mark, who had clearly revised the entire Atlas in preparation, to Tony whose enthusiasm was not matched by his powers of recall. A typical Tony effort going along the lines of ....

"Tony it's your go it's a "C""

"Chad"

"No we've had that try another"

"Cairo"

"That's a city"

"Constantinople"

"That's another city and it doesn't exist anymore it's called Istanbul"

"Canary Islands"

“They are part of Spain”
“It’s the same as Scotland being part of Great Britain, they’re still a country”
Deep sighs follow “Go on then it’ll do. Mark your go”

By the time we reached the edge of Great Wood we are collectively at “F”, losing the will to live and to compound my declining humour a blister on the sole of my foot burst causing me to slow considerably and be in some discomfort for the remainder of the walk. We abandoned countries and attempted a brief foray into “animals” which proved to have even more scope for debate and cheating than “countries”. We really hadn’t found a useful respite from mono syllabic tramping in our intellectual jousting.

The route we were following took us directly past Lord Darnley’s Mausoleum which was in a truly tragic state of dereliction. It was clearly once a special piece of architecture but as a lay person it is hard to believe it could be restored now, certainly not without a vast amount of money. I do remember it being a candidate on BBC2’s restoration program and according to a recent report it has now received a good share of a multi million pound grant to restore it to former glories.
It certainly deserves it; completed in 1784 it was designed by the day’s most trendy architect James Wyatt. Wyatt based his design on the twin foundations of a substantial commission from Lord Darnley and the tomb of King Mausolus at Halicarnassus (now Bodrum in Turkey). Taking offence at the design and origin of the building as being far too overtly pagan the then Bishop of Rochester refused to consecrate it and so it has never been occupied. Seems odd really because the place does have a feeling of

death and decay, perhaps simply because of the state of ruin of the building, and it is a surprise to not find that a 300 year old Darnley family member or two is entombed within. My wife claims it was widely known locally as a place of black magic worship so maybe there is more death in the area than conventional historians have led us to believe.
Let's hope that the restoration of the building goes ahead it is horrible to see something of such unique heritage crumble literally to dust. It would be preserving more than one piece of history of course as old Mausolus's tomb built in 351BC has long since vanished.

Having left the Mausoleum* our route took us round the back of Rochester and Cobham Park Golf Course and on to Shorne country Park. Sadly the country park café had closed by this time but we still stopped for a reviving nip of whisky and to munch through any remaining sugar filled goodies including jelly babies, jaffa cakes, snickers bar, homemade flap jack and cold coffee with about twenty seven spoons of sugar in it.

I am not sure any of that lot made you feel better or worse, especially as jelly babies had become something of a team theme. After six miles the proffered jelly babies seemed like an excellent sugar spike come pick me up but after being offered them every three miles for the next twenty or so they leave you feeling ever so slightly nauseous. No not nauseous, downright sick actually.

*Since the time of writing the Mausoleum has been almost fully restored although as of going to press not yet open to public view.

Our last restart left us with a three mile trudge to home and the welcome relief of removing boots. Three miles is still enough to inflict some sharp reminders that we were not yet in Caledonian Challenge shape. The route wandered through Shorne Country Park which was pleasant enough. This being a regular haunt of Fergus he couldn't understand why he was still on his lead. A regular trip round Shorne gives him ample scope to display his almost limitless stupidity and believe me has lots of it and never tires of demonstrating it. He has three favourite tricks.

1. He would like to swim in the dog pond but is scared of water. As a substitute he runs manically up to the edge of the pond and barks at the pond ferociously doubling his volume if Fiona (my daughter) throws a stick in the pond for him to fetch, or not as the case might be.
2. Especially in the evening he likes to chase rabbits. Mostly this involves him running down a path after the rabbit which dives into the hedge. Fergus continues in a straight line for another hundred yards or so until he returns panting heavily wondering where the rabbit went.
3. There is a variation on the rabbit theme with squirrels. Assuming he actually spots the squirrel running up a tree he then stands at the bottom and springs in the air of all four feet at the same time. He can manage a good foot of vertical travel barely enough to trouble even the most paranoid squirrel.

If you want to picture my dog just think of the donkey from Shrek, he could be his double. I've never checked but I would bet money the animations of the donkey are copied from the antics of a wheaten terrier.
Leaving the country park the last two miles were absolute drudge. The first mile committed us to trudging across a very muddy field. The kind of mud that glues itself to your boots and adds about a pound of unwanted ballast to each step. The last mile was back on pavements through Gravesend which is never fun. As soon as tired feet start connecting with tarmac or concrete they feel hotter and more bothered than they have done all day.
Eventually of course by the simple expedient of putting one foot in front of the other we arrived at home and removed the irksome boots.
I didn't feel too bad, the legs were great, but my feet were mince. A burst blister on each foot was testament to the fact that I needed some more miles in my bag if the Caledonian Challenge itself was not to turn into a very miserable outing.

I tested the rest of the reactions on Monday with an email shot:

> **From:** Jackson, Iain
> **Sent:** 06 February 2006 11:16
> **To:** James Pilcher; john.milner; Paul.martin; Tony.Kennedy
> **Subject:** Sore feet
>
> **Although otherwise completely fine I have managed to collect a couple of nasty blisters, I am less sceptical about taping my feet now**

will try that next time. I am also now allergic to jelly babies and to any form of quiz relating to the countries of the world beginning with letters A-F (inclusive). How is everyone else?

Cheers

Iain

James was the first to reply and as expected in good fettle

From: James Pilcher
Sent: 06 February 2006 11:28
To: Jackson, Iain; john.milner; Paul.martin; Tony.Kennedy
Subject: RE: Sore feet

Hello All,
My feet ached badly once I had sat down for a cup of tea before racing off to get the car. But, I took the dog for a walk on my return and the feet suddenly felt ok...so the message is 'keep walking ' ! Apart from that and a sore left ball...foot that is...no ill effects; but I do feel quite tired today.
Still don't know why razor shark wasn't allowed !
I thought we were pretty mad when we took on this challenge last year. I now think we are completely bonkers !!!!!!!!!!!!!!!!!
See you soon
James

But it had to be Paul to really sum up the day

From: paul.martin
Sent: 06 February 2006 11:00
To: Jackson, Iain
Cc: andy.parr; john.milner James Pilcher; Tony Kennedy
Subject: RE: Sunday

The Stiff Little Fingers song "Sunday Bloody Sunday" keeps limping to mind
- but it's not only my fingers that are stiff today.

Iain, thanks for organising the longest walk i've ever experienced - excellent direction, fantastic country side and great company. But boy do i hurt today, i barely rolled out of bed, then stumbled pitifully to the train station and subsequently shuffled, like a tramp, up the Strand to work in at least 3 * the time it usually takes. Had to buy some more ibuprofen on the way into work.

Much harder work than the 20 miler and i hope yesterday was more typical of the topography of the CC.

Regards

Paul Martin

Charles Taylor Consulting

So the final score for this one 26.2 miles, 800m of climbing very nearly half a Caledonian Challenge, progress of some sort at least.

A Nasty Encounter

The next step in our planned progression and development was to get a bit more used to night hiking. As mentioned earlier I am a big fan of night hiking, it representing practically the only way to get a real feeling of wilderness into walking around the Kent countryside. A twenty mile circular route was planned for a Friday evening taking in detours to refuel with fish and chips and hopefully a beer in our favourite hostellery The Cock at Luddesdowne.*
Paul wimped out claiming a strained medial ligament in his knee. Since the diagnosis for said strained ligament had been dished out by a GP I seriously doubted its accuracy. No disrespect to the great and the good who perform the front line duties of the national health service but I've personally found that muscular/skeletal sports injuries are not really their strong point.

*Note to self: In the unlikely event this ever gets published remember to ask for free beer at "the Cock" for all the free publicity they've had.

Whilst playing bridge the evening before the much more informed partnership of Pilcher/Jackson decided Paul had in fact the much less severe condition of a "sore knee" and rather than rest (as recommended by the GP) he ought to bloody well get on with it. Mind you our opinion had been reinforced by drinking the better part of a bottle of red wine each.

So this time we were five, six counting the faithful hound Fergus. We departed from James's house around six thirty and wandered through Gravesend in the last of the twilight heading out towards Meopham. I knew that in order to detour to the fish and chip shop we had to leave the footpath and walk a short way along the main road before we connected with pavement in Meopham itself. I really wasn't keen on this, the road is pretty busy and although not that narrow I knew we had to keep very close in and keep Fergus on a very short lead. I had driven this way several times on the way home from work and on each occasion pondered whether it was really safe to walk along this bit of road in the dark. Something spooked me about it, I just wasn't happy with the prospect.

As we arrived at the decision point there was a clear consensus to detour as almost no one had eaten (Mark being the exception he had devoured 3 portions of spag bog before leaving home). I lectured everyone about the need for caution, made sure we all had head torches switched on and really thought no more about it.

I was at the front with Fergus and sticking as close as I could to the verge wandered off, on the right side of the road facing the oncoming traffic. A few cars went past without incident and about half way along the 300 yards or so without pavement it nearly turned very nasty.

I remember thinking "crikey he is close", then "well at least he is past me" and then there was a huge thud and a massive pain in my arm and I was lying on the verge at the side of the road. I was absolutely certain I'd broken my arm and equally certain I'd been hit by a wing mirror, on what transpired to be a passing van. Even though it is a couple of months since the incident I can still very accurately remember the sequence of events, and he definitely passed me before he hit me. Obviously this isn't a bad memory failure on my part, more that Einstein didn't get it right after all.

It was a bit chaotic at this point; I was sort of lying there pathetically. Tony was trying to phone for an ambulance who had no idea where Meopham was and without the number of the "A" road (which of course no one knew) the driver needed blow by blow directions from Gravesend. Fergus was stood like a lemon in the middle of the road. Fortunately James grabbed him before he got run over as well.

A few kind souls did stop on the opposite side of the road to check whether anything could be done and after a few minutes the van driver reappeared (to his credit) to check if I was OK. It was at this point after a couple of minutes of lying uselessly in the ditch and holding my arm that I suddenly realised it wasn't broken after all. It was extraordinarily strange. In a split second I went from an absolute certainty that it was broken to an equal and opposite certainty that it wasn't.

I sat up rubbed my arm thoughtfully, got Tony to cancel the ambulance, stood up, found the wing mirror from the van (which had been torn clean off the van door) and prepared to move on.

There was bit of rumbling about giving up but to be honest it was never really a serious option. My arm hurt quite a bit, and I was to say the least a bit pissed off, but I never really thought about giving up.

We wandered off to Meopham fish and chip shop. Someone went off to get my fish and chips whilst I went into the still open Spar to buy an industrial quantity of Nurofen.

Wonder drug Nurofen, it will cure anything from a common cold to a completely severed head. OK so the severed head thing is an exaggeration but it really works wonders for all kinds of rugby related injuries and can also put a serious dent in even the most crippling hang over. Don't take this as advice because I'm pretty sure in the wrong circumstances it could prove fatal. Two Nurofen taken immediately before bed time in partnership with three pints of ice cold water can prevent the occurrence of the impending hang over from hell even after very serious drinking.

I took four (more inappropriate medical behaviour here, never ever deviate from the advice on the packet) and ate my fish and chips in a very subdued manner. My heart wasn't really in this but with a strong Scottish Presbyterian upbringing years of conditioning don't allow me to give up on things.

We moved on, walked up through Camer Park and headed due west on one of the few footpaths in the area of Camer I didn't know well. This is always a problem at night. If you don't know the specifics of the paths you are on you have to be very precise with navigation. Precision at this particular moment wasn't really part of my agenda, my arm hurt too much.

As a result we took a wrong turning, couldn't really describe it as lost as I knew pretty much where I had gone wrong but it took a little bit of sorting out where we were when the footpath eventually connected with the road. Worse than that, we were now very tight for time to get to the Cock for last orders. This evening really wasn't panning out as I'd hoped.

A bloody miserable trudge back up the Weald way got us back to Luddesdowne about ten to eleven. Thankfully the kind peoples of the Cock served us and as ever the beer was excellent. I'd really had enough of the evening though, not even a really great pint of Adnams Broadside revived my flagging spirits. My suggestion to bag it for the day was greeted uniformly with approval and we headed off to Gravesend a pretty weary bunch.

A nasty experience seems to drain the body of energy and it seemed like everyone had extra miles in their legs as we trudged the last mile or two along deserted streets back to home.

All things considered it wasn't too bad in the end, we managed 18 miles in 6 and half hours of darkness, including a stop for fish and chips and a rapidly drunk beer. Oh I nearly forgot we lost a few minutes looking for someone's wing mirror.

More pain and Gain

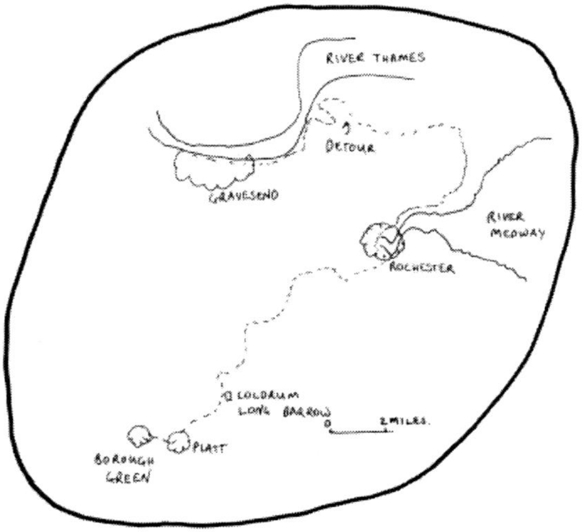

The good people who organise the Caledonian Challenge recommended a training schedule that included one long walk, the prescribed distance a breezy 35 miles. More judicious use of memory map saw me plan a route encompassing a reasonably beefy amount of North Downs and then finishing with the reverse of the Christmas walk along the Medway and back along the Thames.
The rubber was starting to meet the road now and the Whisky Club internal rumour mill was working over time. Paul was hesitant to commit. He wasn't replying to email and direct questioning solicited only vague and evasive responses. To boot he had just started a mammoth garden landscaping project that involved digging up most of Kent to facilitate the building of three separate patios. I didn't quite get the hang of why anyone would want three patios

but it seemed like as a minimum it should provide some extra training. That was until Paul's back gave out and he had to have it strapped with about three miles of tape from his physio. Underlying all of that though was the rumour that he was looking to miss the thirty five miles in case it proved too much, injured him, caused his dodgy knee to flare up or otherwise provided incontrovertible evidence that fifty four miles would be a bridge too far.

In a way I could sort of related to his reasoning. Having got this far maybe the best chance of success laid in saving everything for one big push on the day. For the team though we undoubtedly wanted him to complete the training walk. If the aforementioned evidence of impending failure did indeed lie just below the surface then much better to surface it now than during the actual event.

Some gentle pressure, and reassuring advice from the physio that walking was good for a bad back (cost me a few quid to get the physio to sign up to that particular advice) won the day and in due course the email arrived in my inbox confirming participation. Once again we were complete, six walkers plus Fergus the dog ready to circumnavigate Kent for no particular purpose other than filling a random Saturday and proving that age is no barrier to acts of self indulgent madness.

The start point this time was in Borough Green and having experienced the nasty end of driving a car there (i.e. picking it up after the walk when completely shagged) this time Tony had booked us a cab. At some ungodly hour of the morning (5:30 am if I remember correctly) we assembled at Tony's house and bundled into the waiting cab. Fergus was less than happy about the process. He is fine in the boot of my Honda but inside a car he gets very nervous. When he sits on the back seat with my daughter

Fiona he leans on her so hard he squashes her into a tiny corner. Now he had decided he wanted to sit on my lap in the back of the cab which would have been approximately as difficult as holding a very large, slimy, flapping fish on my lap. He doesn't just want to sit there he wants to climb inside my shirt presumably as some sort of weird dog comforter. Anyway with six of us crammed into the people carrier there wasn't room for him on my lap so I held him firmly down in an act of inestimable cruelty and he finally resigned himself to sitting on the floor. He behaved pretty well for the rest of the journey and only launched two hundred and seventy six missions (all failed) to get on my lap during the thirty minute trip to Borough Green.

Like all of the walks (Xmas snow was the exception) the first part of the walk was extremely pleasant. As you leave Borough Green you pass almost immediately through the very pretty village of Platt which is clearly home to some punters with serious wedge. There were some fantastic and immaculately kept houses; in fact what struck you most was that there really wasn't anything remotely out of place in the whole village. It felt like the quintessential English village especially manicured for the day to be photographed and made into countless postcards and jigsaw puzzles. English villages are possessors of some really unique atmosphere and on a sunny day there is nothing finer to observe village life than to sit outside the pub with a glass of proper beer watching the cricket on the village green. It is a picture hard to transport outside of England. Trying to explain the simultaneous joys of warm beer and cricket to an American or a continental European is a task far beyond my limited use of the English language. Even those, like the Aussies, who have a passing understanding of cricket, sort of glaze over if you try to explain why it would be a good idea to drink warm beer on a blazing hot summer's day. We sauntered on discussing mostly how at times the world's economies are awash with cash and how the hell do you tap into it to buy your own bit of English idyll. No one had much of a solution with the prevailing opinions split on how the residents of Platt came by their respective large wedges. The two camps divided neatly into "old money" (they've always been rich and idle) and "new money" (city bonuses are obscene). Unfortunately none of us fall into either camp and I seriously doubt enough of you will read this book (assuming it ever gets published which is unlikely) for me to join the new money camp and buy my own country estate.

The route we were following now headed north and joined The Weald Way. We had used other parts of the Weald Way in training, it provides a route around the South East from Gravesend to Eastbourne. The Weald Way along with the North Downs Way and the Saxon Shore Way had been integral to finding reasonably long but navigationally easy routes to train on. Trying to connect lots of minor footpaths can lead to a lot of map checking and it drags out the whole enterprise. It is much easier to bang along a major footpath following little posts with arrows and WW markers on them.

It seemed that there was a theme of death about our rambles round Kent. Following more than one walk past Lord Darnley's mausoleum we now found ourselves by Coldrum long barrow. This time we did stop for a nose around. Superficially it is just some big stones plonked on the ground but devotees of this kind of artefact wax lyrical about Coldrum. Some brief forays into Google yielded a web site where there were even star ratings for various long barrow's, Coldrum I think was a five star long barrow so it

had to be worth a look
Star ratings seemed a bit over the top but I do find this kind of ancient structure fascinating mostly because it is easy to imagine the sheer scale of the human endeavour needed to construct one. The organisation needed to bring just manual labour to bear on the task is pretty impressive. If you stand next to one of the main stones it is difficult to imagine how it can ever be man handled into place.
The National Trust plaque marking the site contained all the information I could ever want about Coldrum long barrow. I learned that it was constructed sometime in the third millennium BC an impossibly long time ago. It is hard to cast your mind over such a huge space of time. Someone once told me that the human perception of number usually ends at about the number seven. Throw a number of objects on a table and without stopping to count them most people are reasonably accurate in telling you how many there are up to the number seven. Beyond that there is a very rapid drop off so our number perception of one million, ten million or one hundred million is limited to them all being incomprehensibly big numbers. 3000BC has much the same effect on me, I know it is a very long time ago but I am not connected to it being any further in the past than say 300AD. Suffice it to say there were a lot of dead people ensconced there a very long time ago. It does make you wonder how they lived in 3000BC clearly there was enough of a structure to their society to gather them together to build this burial chamber. It was equally hard to visualise the landscape of five thousand years ago. From my limited knowledge I am guessing everything would have been forested and populated not just by the builders of long barrows but by various long extinct animals such as wolves and bears.

My curiosity was tweaked by my visit and in an effort to put into context how old this place was I did some more googling and put it in my terms it fitted in significant history roughly as follows

About 40000 years ago we had Neanderthal man
About 14000 years ago the last Ice Age ended
About 7000 years ago first signs of what I know as "Stone Age" man appeared and he had some basic stone tools and some signs of farming.
About 4000 years ago the Bronze Age started.
Right after that someone built Coldrum Long Barrow about a thousand years before Stonehenge and about three thousand years before the battle of Hastings. (The only date in the whole of history I ever managed to consign to memory).

It is actually quite a peaceful; spot and since it can only be reached on foot probably doesn't get that many visitors. It certainly doesn't have the same feeling of decay and dilapidation evident from a visit to the Mausoleum. The architecture of the mausoleum needs active preservation to prevent it falling into an ugly state of disrepair. I have the impression that if left to its own devices Coldrum long Barrow by contrast would melt slowly and with dignity back into the landscape so that in another few thousand years it was returned to nature.

Shortly after this we transitioned from Weald Way to North Downs way and ascended to the top of the downs. This was a fairly long pull amply rewarded by fine views of the Weald of Kent. If you want a view of the patchwork fields of England then the top of the Downs is a good place to be.

Laid out before us was a patchwork of green fields not yet quite destroyed by the ugly yellow sported by oil seed rape. This stuff is grown everywhere in our proximity and apart from having vicious pollen that starts the most appalling hay fever I find its garish yellow hard on the eye and out of place in the softer colours of a traditional English landscape. I am sure it is probably only grown because of some obscene EEC subsidy.
The European Common Agricultural Policy has a lot to answer to. Apart from the headline grabbing generation of wine Lakes and Butter Mountains it seems able to create ways of distributing huge amounts of cash for purposes other than effective growing and rearing of food. My own favourite tale of how the policy works was of the Italian cattle farmers. Having offered subsidies that created a vast excess of milk and dairy produce the policy went into reverse and offered a bounty for each slaughtered dairy cow. Proof of slaughter was to be made by sending an ear from the slaughtered beast to the appropriate body. Lots of Italian hill farmers allegedly availed themselves of this policy and were simultaneously the owners of large herds of strange one eared cattle. I can't remember if anyone ever worked out the rouse, probably not I would guess.
Mercifully today the rape was not yet in full flower so it spared us the need for tinted glasses to view the landscape and spared me a substantial amount of sneezing.

Having crested the Downs our route wandered towards Rochester. It was pleasant enough going taking us through Horseholders Wood and Wingate Wood eventually out into the village of Cuxton. This was our first stop. In an effort to emulate the real event we planned stops based on distance. We would stop at 12 miles, then 24 miles and ignore the normal practice of stopping for lunch and tea. So arriving at Cuxton we had reached the twelve mile mark and stopped for a refuelling stop and a change of socks.

Feet get disproportionately hot on walks, mine having the better part of nineteen stone landing on them were kicking up already. Fresh socks certainly helped at least for a mile afterwards my feet felt pretty well. At the 12 mile mark though hot spots on the feet meant a portent of blisters to come and I knew I was going to have trouble later on.

The other key issue for the day was food. Being the irascible pedant I know I am, and having dictated we should aim for stops of no more than twenty minutes, everyone was trying vainly to stuff down an appropriate amount of food and water. By the time you've messed about changing socks and stopped for a piss there isn't much of twenty minutes left. On a day that would see us walking for at least twelve hours you need some reasonable sustenance and we were majoring on sugar loaded Mars bars and cake. I am no physiologist but to my limited understanding this is a stupendously bad idea. The body digests all of the sugar very quickly and sends a huge spike of sugar into the blood stream. This has the short term benefit of giving you a lift and energising you, however it won't last. In a vainglorious attempt to keep everything balanced the body responds by injecting a large dose of insulin into the blood stream which causes the blood sugar to crash and leaves you feeling tired and crap. If you respond by eating more sugar the whole process will begin again but with more extreme spikes and crashes. Eventually you will descend into a horrible mess as your blood sugar wildly oscillates and your system is no longer sure if it is on a high or a low.

If you want to see an image of what is happening to your

system look for The Tacoma Narrows Bridge on Google and you can find the film of the wobbly bridge that self destructed in the wind. It is only a short leap of imagination to extrapolate your internal machinations forced by consumption of so much crappy food.

So suitably sustained or not we carried on to Rochester. Tony was decidedly struggling already and was feeling the start of blisters on both feet. Once you feel the start of blisters you have to deal with them. Leave them and they get bigger and bigger until eventually they burst and trust me that hurts, a lot!

As a largely unsympathetic lot we left Tony to patch his feet (with John) and wandered off for a brief look around the castle.

The castle as it stands today dates from just after the Norman conquest (1066 see I can still remember that date). It seems to have a history steeped in folks with comical names its constructor being one Bishop Gundulf clearly on loan from an appearance in some Tolkeinesque epic. Other early characters included King William Rufus and some guy called Odo. I'd swear someone was making these up but it seems not as several different sources affirm their existence.

The early part of the castles history is convoluted with its ownership and construction the subject of much turmoil. Throw in a few mediaeval sieges and you'll capture the early history pretty well.

What everyone seems to agree on is that around 1087 the ownership of the castle fell to Bishop Gundulf who rebuilt the castle at his own expense out of stone. The cost of the castle amounted to £60 about the cost of a round of beers in a trendy London bar now.

I like the castle a lot. Although it is in quite a bad state it feels like a castle should. Great thick stone walls that you can imagine withstanding infinite poundings and indeed there are numerous accounts of the castles longevity under severe attack. Its level of decay is appropriate for its age, it seems to have faded gracefully and kept its essential character even though gently crumbling at the edges. I tried to pin down why the castle is full of character and Lord Darnley's mausoleum is an ugly eye sore. It's not just the huge metal fence around the Mausoleum it's about appropriate conservation. It isn't necessary to fully restore something to recover its character but it can't look derelict. Lord Darnely's mausoleum looks abandoned and unloved, Rochester castle is more like a favourite aunt, a little old round the edges but still full of character and with more than a tale or two to tell.

Well wandering round the castle wasn't going to get us anywhere and by this time with John's assistance Tony had patched up his blistered feet and we pressed on. We re-crossed the Medway this time by the road bridge in the middle of Rochester and rounding the edge of Strood headed for Upnor.

I managed to acquire a new pub fact something I hadn't realised possible as I thought I knew all there was to know about pubs. The pub on the outskirts of Strood was flying a Rainbow flag one which John asserted indicated it was a gay pub, or at least a pub in which members of the gay community like to drink, as I'm not certain a building can posses a given sexuality or indeed state of happiness or misery.

The route now became familiar as we were walking back along the route we had followed five months previously during our first proper training outing over Xmas. The route took us through Upnor and back over the Hoo peninsula to the RSPB reserve at High Halstow.

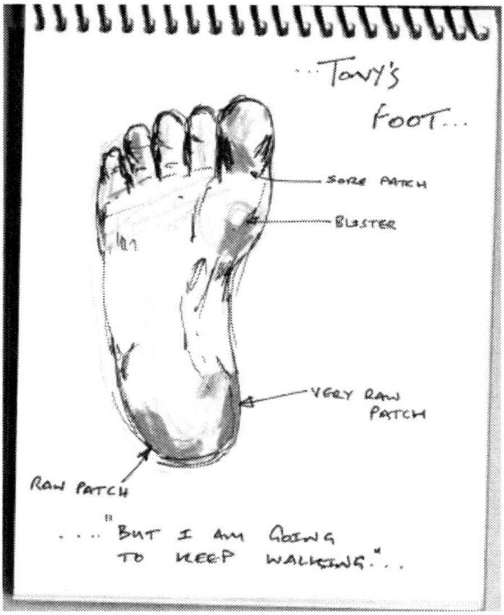

We met our extended support crew at High Halstow this time consisting of four dogs, four adults and five children. A brief stop at the rendezvous began to reveal the full extent of damage inflicted on several of our number. The consistent theme was feet. Sore feet, blistered feet, hot feet and by far the worst, Tony's feet. The blisters that first emerged at Rochester had reached significant proportions and were clearly causing him trouble. His decision to switch to shoes rather than stick to boots was precipitated more out of hope than expectation. In fact with blisters on the soles of his feet, more a result of constant pounding than any boot or shoe rubbing, the thinner sole of his walking shoe would offer less rather than more protection. One guarantee about Tony, he isn't a whinger. We rounded everyone up and headed off. Our pace now matched perfectly to the extended herd we had. We were definitely much slower than earlier and sauntered reasonably happily along at the pace of the kids we had in tow.

We detoured at Cooling for those that hadn't yet seen them to briefly study the Dickensian gravestones: Of more interest though seemed to be the very in vogue pastime of celebrity spotting and rowing merrily along his private lake was one Mr. Jools Holland. Apparently he owns and is some time resident of Cooling Castle. For no other reason than we expected he had loads of money various people were put up to asking him to serve us some nice tea and scones. I don't think we would have received a polite response; we left him enjoying his Sunday afternoon paddle and headed off to Cliffe.

The extended group repaired happily to the cars and the six of us plus Fergus headed off for the last leg along the river to Gravesend. Fergus seemed less than thrilled by the prospect and made several bids to leap into the back of the car and ride home. No such luck, he was part of the walking crew like it or lump it and I dragged him by his lead round the corner and off onto the last leg. Damn it if I was going to walk the last leg he bloody well was too.

Looking back it is very hard to describe the mind set on these long drags. One almost starts to hallucinate or alternatively falls into long rambling musings about the most irrelevant rubbish. Such a frame of mind led to a long debate about how Mark could be more fully occupied as a member of our team. Clearly this whole exercise was trivially easy for him and we needed to make better use of his spare horsepower. The team embarked on a project of how to best use Mark starting with a few essentials he could carry for us.

Some of the basics needed on such an adventure like a keg of cold lager and a few nice snacky things. Our imagination though started to get the better of us and we started to design ever more complicated mechanisms for Dickins to help us out. In the end we settled for him backpacking a small shed we could take turns to rest in. Oh and wouldn't it be nice if he could include a few features inside like chilled lager on tap, sky sports on the telly and maybe an attractive girly or two to serve the drinks. Perhaps not. Bitter experience has told me many times that fatigue and navigation duties are not a healthy mix. It is a hard lesson to learn though. Apparently one of the differentiating capabilities of human over animal is his or hers ability to learn from experience and apply it to the future. Certainly doesn't apply to drinking whisky though. Experience has told me an excess the drinking thereof will lead to a very unpleasant morning after. Doesn't seem to have modulated my behaviour one bit and I continue to singularly fail in the task of associating excess whisky with near death experiences (death seems preferable on occasions) the following morning.

I'm afraid the need to double and triple check navigation details when knackered falls into the same category. I've made countless errors like this resulting in spectacular detours, ascending back up the mountain when I'm supposed to be descending, a round tour of the forest near Betws-Y-Coed which should have left us six miles from Betws on our way up some mountain. It actually left us near the village signpost (famously identified with the cry from the walking group of "We'll know where we are now!") which on close examination revealed the village name Betws-Y-Coed.

Have I learnt anything? Not a scrap. This time I didn't even check the map, just followed the biggest path and assumed we were going the right way. A strange feeling of uneasiness gradually evolved into a sense of doom that we were definitely not on the path we had been at Xmas. Reluctantly at this point I had to accept that all was not well and check the map. Careful study (i.e. a casual glance) revealed we were almost certainly on the wrong side of Cliffe creek and had just added two and half miles of additional and entirely unnecessary detour to the walk. Of course although my brain was 100% certain of this my body refused to accept it and so we sent Mark, our only truly able bodied soul at this point, up ahead to peer over the sea wall and relay the hoped for information that we were on course and had a few hundred yards to go to Cliffe Fort. Bollocks!

We were of course on the wrong side of Cliffe creek and had a mile inland to round the head of the creek and a mile back up the creek to Cliffe fort all of two hundred yards away. All entirely avoidable if I had navigated properly and followed the correct path that goes directly from Cliffe, across the head of the creek to Cliffe Fort.

In fairness no one moaned, much. Mark aside (bastard I hate him) everyone was struggling quite a bit. James looked washed out. Paul had slowed to a pace reminiscent of a very slow sloth hobbling around the rainforest floor on a bad Monday morning after an especially heavy weekend of sloth partying on the fermenting fruits of the forest.

Tony was in pain. Not discomfort pain. His face was grimacing. His permanent optimism and associated incessant chatter had reduced to an occasional grunt.

I felt bad that I had added a good 45 minutes of extra walking to the whole enterprise but secretly good that I didn't feel too bad physically. There was always a degree of internal competition between us and in the whole six months of training and attempting the Caledonian challenge this was probably my high point in terms of my fitness and durability. Mark apart I was clearly in the best shape.

I gloated a little, strode out a bit and made for home. (Oops must mention here Fergus was absolutely fine he'll never forgive me if I don't give him due credit for his indestructibility).
Well we made it somehow. The last three miles were not fun. We had however walked 37 miles and it had taken 14 hours. If this was the cally challenge we would have 17 miles to go and ten hours left to do it. I felt OK. Everyone was in pretty bad order but surely we could limp, hop, crawl, carry, drag or otherwise self propel the team round a further 17 miles in ten hours?

I slumped in a chair as soon as I could remove my boots and drew a long draught of a cold isotonic Stella. Fergus by contrast slumped only briefly before rushing out the door at high speed to bark at next doors dog.

Team training was over. The next time we donned boots, gathered our will power and collectively marched over the horizon would be the 16th June 2006, 7am, Fort William.

Just Getting to The Start Line.........

Even Paul was now becoming optimistic and fit. His email review of the 37 miler had been positive and upbeat without the one week long recuperation needed after previous efforts.

From: Paul Martin
Sent: 2 May 2006
To: Iain Jackson
Subject: Re: Saturday

Iain, Thanks once again for organising and dragging us along in yours and Ferg's (the real man of the day) wake. This turned out to be a hard walk and to all those that breezed the 27 miler a good reminder that blisters, inadequate food and drink can take its toll. I even managed a bit of digging yesterday so some positives and hopefully the shuffling 80 year that I became after previous walks is now a thing of the past with the Jackson training regime.

The last drag along the Thames was a real "road to perdition" - a place or state of pain or suffering...........glad that it is over.

Looking forward to the debrief and logistics discussion Wednesday.

Cheers

Paul Martin

Life of course is never ever simple. It had been great fun and at times hard work getting this far and we felt if not fully prepared at least in with a very good shout of putting

up a creditable performance. Not that we were a creditable performance sort of a team. All of the characters in our team were finish or die sort of people and the goal was very clearly defined. Finish as a team in 23 hours 59 minutes and 59 seconds equals happiness. Anything else equals abject failure, misery and self loathing in equal measures.

The final training walk had been on the 29th April and D-Day was on the 16th June so we had a few weeks left to keep ourselves active and fit. Everyone seemed to find their own way through this part of the exercise. Paul as mentioned had embarked on a landscape gardening project roughly equal in scale to the restoration of the Lost Gardens of Helligan

and had enlisted Mark as his chief navy/bricky/technical consultant. Mind you Mark annoyingly could have spent the intervening four weeks engaged in a hedonistic orgy of barbecue and beer and still been by far the most able of us at the start line.

Almost all fitness and diet web sites and self help books tend to ignore one blindingly obvious fact. Genetics plays a huge role. Sure if you've got good genes a crap life style can still turn you into Homer Simpson but if you've got outstanding genes you have to work really hard at slobbish behaviour to not have at least a pretty good athletic ability. If by contrast you've got really crap genes then the slightest deviation from the "you are what you eat" diet turns you immediately into Mr. Blobby. I always preach separating facts from opinion and these are definitely facts. Don't listen to all the diet doctors telling you "you are what you eat" in fact "you are what you are" (mostly) so live with it.

James had set himself on a few runs, Tony was majoring in dog walking and I was engaged in my usual mix of mountain biking, running round the forest and dog walking. I was trying (but failing) to shed a few vital kilos before the event. I weighed 19stone 3lbs when I left University and at the start line I weighed 19st 2lbs. As I write this my last medical told me I had to lose six stone, I'm searching on line for the chain saw store to buy the equipment needed to amputate a leg as that's the only way I ever reach 13 stone.

We also had quite clearly not put enough energy into the logistics. Since some time back David had indicated his preference not to drive us around Scotland and spend one night with zero sleep. He had been replaced on the driving list by my wife Alison and James's wife Christine. The circumstance for their volunteering however needs some elucidation.

For some years now we have been playing bridge as a four. I'm supposed to be teaching them how to play but it's hard when sufficient alcohol is drunk every week, during and after card playing, to erase all the memory cells that stored the useful bridge knowledge. The consequence of the alcohol consumption is three fold:

1. Everyone has a damn good time.
2. The speed of improvement in assimilating essential bridge know how (such as how many points are needed to open the bidding) is measured on the same scale as drifting continents.
3. Anyone will sign up for anything at the end of the evening including spending two days supporting a group of very tired, grumpy and smelly blokes around Scotland.

Furthermore, and on reflection I have no idea how we concluded this was a good idea, we had decided that the vehicle of choice for the entire party was Tony's Chrysler Voyageur. That's eight people (six walkers two support people) a dog and all their walking kit in a Chrysler voyager. Yes I know it's only a seven seater but the clinching idea that got Tony's car the vote was to place a small wooden plank between two back seats for James to sit on. For eleven hours on a drive from Gravesend to Fort William...........and back........after completing a 54 mile walk.......in twenty four hours. Genius.

We also had the most comprehensive food and first aid kit list imaginable. I tried to get the publisher to add proper appendices listing our kit and food, (all of Chris Bonnington's books have them so why can't mine?). The publisher just laughed and said you can't publish a kit list that major's on beer. Anyway I like lists so just for the record our medical kit was as follows:

Nurofen, Nurofen plus, Compeed blister plasters, rehydration sachets, zinc gauze tape, ordinary plasters, various strappings and bandages, waspeeze, antihistamine tablets, savlon, antiseptic wipes and gaffer tape. Yes that's right a great big roll of silver gaffer tape the same stuff used for fixing up air conditioning systems. If you want to know why gaffer tape features on the kit list read some of the excellent internet articles on ultra running such as the one to be found on http://www.ottawaoutdoors.ca/index.php?option=com_content&task=view&id=83

Our food list was even more impressive and read as follows:

Two dozen eggs
HP sauce
Heinz tomato ketchup
48 bread rolls
Jumbo boxes of cereal bars
Six packets of oat cakes
Lots and lots of bananas
Strawberries (allegedly they contain some chemical that helps to improve mood)
Eight tins of Heinz "big soup" and four tins of lentils to add to it
2lbs cheddar cheese (strong)
Branston pickle
Cooked chicken legs (for Fergus he has to eat too)
Chocolate cake (large)
Boxes and boxes of jaffa cakes and chocolate rolls
Nuts
Rasins
Jam

Peanut butter
Mars bars, chocolate bars, snickers

The flea sized amount of brain power we had applied to the food list was based on the following reasoning. Fried egg sandwiches for 10am stop would as we would have been going for a few hours and was a reasonable mix of protein and slow burning carbs. A main midday meal of soup with added lentils for more slow burning carbs and protein. Snacks of bananas, nuts, cheese rolls or oat cakes for most of the day again the idea was to fuel with some complex and slow release carbs. Chocolate cake for the last stop in the middle of the night for a much needed sugar and caffeine boost to push us on to the finishing line, or at least we hoped it would be a push for the finish and not a solace for failure.
Last the killer ingredient, strawberries. Whilst hunting for web hints on nutrition (google being the World's primary prevarication vehicle as a work substitute for all desk based employees connected to the internet) I came upon this excellent recipe.

Blues Buster

Mix all ingredients thoroughly on high speed in the blender.
12 oz. of strawberry flavored yogurt
1 small ripe banana
1 Tbs. unsweetened cocoa
4 to 6 frozen strawberries
1 tsp. unflavored or orange flavored cod liver oil
1 tbs. of smooth almond butter (at room temperature)

Optional:
1 Tbs. of honey
1 cup of fresh berries
Yogurt, banana, chocolate and almonds are all "good mood" foods.

It looked so weird having cod liver oil mixed with berries it had to work. A bit too complicated for the real event though and the prospect of burping fish oil for 54 miles was also not too appealing. We decided to keep it simple for the real event and stick to unprocessed strawberries as they promised the highest level of mood enhancing active ingredient and were decidedly more palatable than fish oil.

So now we were ready. Everything was bought we had our logistics in place, kit checks were done nothing could go wrong……..

John however was strangely quiet and the rumour mill had it that all might not be well in the Milner camp. As time marched on I had some back of mind concern that he hadn't fully recovered from the calf niggle that had been bothering him for some time and day dreaming at work (as usual) the bomb shell missive duly arrived.

From: John Milner
Sent: 5 June 2006 18:05
To: Iain Jackson; James Pilcher; Mark Dickins; Tony Kennedy; Paul Martin
Subject: Your new support driver

I have now reluctantly accepted that I won't be walking the challenge. I've been putting off final decision as long as I could. I am waiting for a referral letter to a specialist to look at my calf muscle.

I now need to engage with the logistics side of the walk. What food you all want, medical kit, bags (you can borrow mine) etc rather than my own walk. Perhaps we could have a quick pre meet pre tennis?

My own feeling is I can do the support on my own but there is less risk if we collar one RBS person to do it with me. I think Tony is going to put me on his insurance.

If any piss taking or country naming is required I can provide this at scheduled stops.

Let me know what you think

Cheers

John Milner APMP MRICS
Member for and on behalf of Bailey Garner LLP

So now we were five and a dog and we had solved our driving problem. Alison and Christine were honest enough to say that they were hugely relieved not to have to trek round Scotland and stay up all night supporting us lot. Honestly speaking I was mighty glad we were no longer trying to fit eight people and a dog in a Chrysler voyager as the aforementioned "plank between the seats" scheme was frankly nuts.

The last week before departure seemed interminable, not helped in my case by a last minute business trip to Germany. Finally though Thursday evening arrived and we rendez vous'd on the pavement outside Tony's house with our kit ready to pack the car for an early morning departure. The mountain of kit that sat on the pavement was jaw dropping. Christ it looked like we were off to Everest not for a stroll on a pretty well made footpath. As soon as we started loading the car I knew Fergus was staying at home.

The car was packed with stuff and with six of us in there it was going to be a pretty cramped journey. If we had him inside the car with us it would be a nightmare for us and him all the way to Scotland, it wasn't going to happen. How the Billy Bollocks we thought we were going to get two more people and their kit and Fergus into the car was now incomprehensible. If this was a measure of how well planned we were then it didn't bode well. Fergus to be fair to him took the news of his staying at home rather well and cheerfully rushed off out doors to bark at next door's dog. The 6am departure on Friday would see us to Fort William around 4 pm. The biggest motorway breakfast ever eaten (Paul had the king size fry up with extra grease and devoured the whole lot in 1 minute 23 seconds with the exception of the half a grilled tomato the only remotely healthy element of the whole meal), one copy of Nuts, one of Zoo and two hundred and forty six games of knock out whist later and we did indeed arrive in Fort William at 4pm.

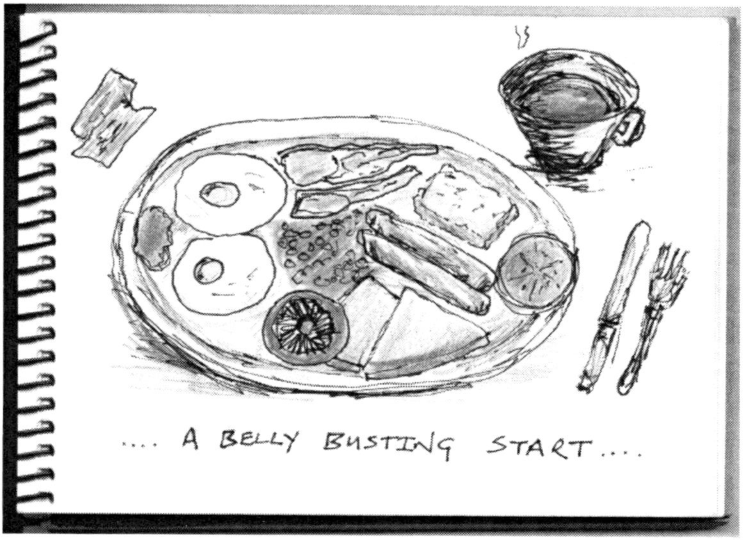

It started to get scary now. It's the same whenever I do one of these damn challenge events. At registration there are hundreds of fit looking types. The type varies according to event. If you run a 10km race you are surrounded by stick thin athletes, compete in an adventure race and there are loads of fit looking muscely triathlon types. Here we were in the midst of literally hundreds of beardy Munro baggers, veterans of thousands of miles of Scottish fell and probably each having climbed the entire list of Munros twice (the 284 mountains in Scotland over 3000′). At every single registration queue there is only one obviously fat bloke. Me. At least on this occasion I could take solace that there was one obviously fat bloke (me) and one slightly fat bloke (Paul). I had to admit though he had done far better than me on the weight loss than me and looked a lot closer to the homogenously fit and lean looking Munro bagging bastards we were surrounded by than I did. As if that wasn't enough we were positively ancient in this company. Our average age came in at a meaty forty three and two fifths, at first glance the average of the rest of the people registering was about twelve. Even accounting for the fact that when you're a grumpy old git everyone looks at least thirty years younger than you the average age couldn't have been more than twenty two. We were toast, what the hell were we thinking about entering this damn event.

These queues always intimidate me. I hate registration for this reason and the sole thought running round and round in my head like a stuck copy of some dreadful record was "What am I doing here?" At least the thought of a stuck record provoked an inward smile as it reminded me that one of Joe Simpson's motivations for staying alive after his accident in Peru was to not die with Brown Girl in the Ring by Boney M going round and round in his head. I don't

think my situation was quite as serious as his.
Well we were here any way so we registered and collected our goodie bags. I didn't know why I bothered with this either to be honest as another recurring theme of me entering challenges and races is that the giveaway T-Shirt (largest size available of course) is always too small.
As an almost throw away after thought we also bought several rolls of army strength zinc oxide tape for taping feet something that was to prove a portentous decision later on in proceedings.

So that was it we were ready. There was just time for fish and chips and a couple of quiet pints in the bar and off to bed for an early night. No going back now the body was prepared, or at least there was no chance to prepare it better in the next seven hours, the success or failure would now exclusively be in the head.

The First Leg Fort William to Kinlochleven.

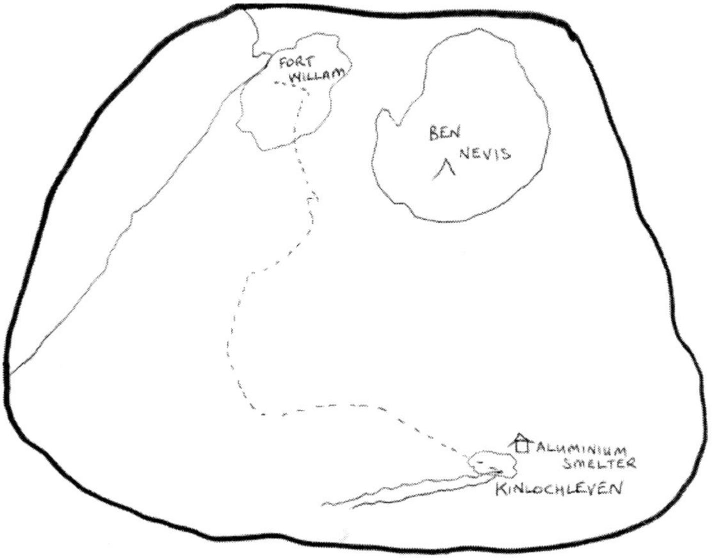

It was 5:00 am and everyone was very quiet. Sitting at the breakfast table trying to consume an industrial quantity of cornflakes was hard work at the best of times but somehow my saliva would not arrive and I just did not feel hungry. Toast was a little more successful and a few slices were forced down. At least after last night's pints I was thirsty and could manage about ten cups of tea. No one else was saying much either and we finished breakfast, had the obligatory nerve induced three dumps each gathered our kit up and convened outside the hotel. It was a grey drizzly damp morning.

The before photograph now makes me smile. Tony looks hysterical, Mark a bit bored, the rest look like condemned

men awaiting the gallows. Well at least everyone looked nervous.
John now took on his role of team “Dad”. I would say without reservation from this moment on that we had the best possible support. I take that back as I did have one reservation. John proceeded to drive Tony’s Chrylser up the forest road to the start as though he was a carbon copy of the late Colin Macrae in a special stage of the GB Rally. Not that I mind fast(ish) driving but the effect on Tony’s Voyageur of being driven over forest road pot holes at 40 mph with four fully grown adults and two substantially overgrown adults as passengers was a bit alarming. Tony, bless him, looked extremely concerned but kept shtum. Despite his best efforts John dropped us at the start the recommended 1 hour before the go gun (6am ugh!!). Of course as usual with these events (I should have known better than to believe the official advice) the one hour in advance recommendation included a time safety margin

sufficient to read War and Peace. There were about twenty people at the start at 6am. The start line was populated by ten officials, five of us and five other walkers naive enough to believe the recommendation that you had to be at the start line by 6am for the starting gun at 7am.

The remaining six hundred and ninety people starting at 7am arrived in dribs and drabs from around 6:20 and then a big rush at almost exactly 6:55.

In the one hour we stood around in the drizzle we had attracted a medium sized collection of midges that were infesting hair, ear and nostrils and drinking a hearty breakfast of fat person blood. At least I thought they were only medium in intensity, Mark ignored them completely (this man really is unbelievable does he feel no pain?). The rest having no previous experience of the midge (Scottish variety) were finding the midges decidedly nasty and had all donned midge nets.

As more and more people arrived of course the collective body heat attracts disproportionately more midges from further afield and they really started to be a damn nuisance. To compensate it started to rain harder which drives away midges but does nothing to raise morale.

Some bloke made a speech. A pretty brave speech as he started out by telling us that the whole stupid idea of the Caledonian Challenge was his. I wasn't sure if the crowd would cheer him or lynch him. Mostly they just stood there looking damp midge bitten and vaguely pissed off. He went on tell us that he had done it many times, that anyone could do it (i.e. if you fail you are clearly a pathetic, weak and infirm representative of the human species). His wife apparently was in a team whose target time was sixteen hours. I pondered long on the question of which form of motorised transport she was going to use to complete 54 miles in sixteen hours. If this was meant to be motivating it completely missed the mark. I wanted to hear that what we were about to embark on was only just a fraction easier than a walk to the South Pole and that our brave and selfless sacrifice would not only raise vast fortunes for Scottish charity but raise us on to a higher spiritual plane where we would bask in a state of self actualization* for the coming six months. Instead I heard that his brother had completed it no problem having only trained by walking to the City of London in black brogues and in the course of said training having removed most of the skin from his feet. So now the bar was even lower. Apparently even an idle city broker with no training and no skin on his feet can do the walk. If we failed we would not just be pathetic weak and infirm but affirmably spineless. Joy.

Thank fully this inspirational soliloquy didn't last too long and to the skirl of the pipes the starting gun went and we were off. It was by now raining pretty steadily and we trudged off up a gentle gradient passed the assembled pipe band (who did a passing impersonation of a damp, midge bitten and vaguely pissed off pipe band) and we were on our way.

Fort William, the starting point for the walk, I've always found to be a rather disappointing town. I searched a bit on line for the descriptions of Fort William and mostly they are pretty accurate. They refrain from describing it as a quaint market town nestling under the majestic slopes of Ben Nevis and settle for something altogether more prosaic. Fort William "on line" comes up with "*Fort William is*

- *See Maslow's hierarchy of needs for an explanation.

the largest town in the west Highlands of Scotland and is the commercial centre of Lochaber, an area renowned for magnificent scenery with an important history."

It's hardly advertising for hoards of tourist to day trip to Fort William and with good reason.

I have a bit more practical view of the place it is a bit of a dump but in a brilliant location. The town is grey and on a rainy day thoroughly unattractive. The town centre verges on the grubby and is useful for practical matters like buying groceries or finding an Indian restaurant. Matters not easily serviced in the rest of the area.

Lochaber though, the district Fort William is the centre of, is magnificent.

Ben Nevis the highest mountain in Britain is a vast mass of rocky crags and gullies and on a smaller scale competes in grandeur with any alpine rock face.

Fort William is also located within a short drive of some well known and some less well known places of beauty.

My own personal favourite some fifty seven miles drive from Fort William is the small summit of Meall Sanna. I won't tell you where it is but if you bother to find it on a map, visit it, and enjoy the view facing due West then I guarantee you will thank me for the information. In the interests of full disclosure I should also point out I spent many summer holidays here as a small boy and that my grandparents come from this area but it doesn't bias my opinion one bit. I've been there with many well travelled people, most recently my wife and daughter, and every single person proclaims it one of the most beautiful spots they have ever visited. I can also guarantee the view from here; the same cannot be said for Ben Nevis. Apparently the summit of Ben Nevis is free from cloud on average only 60 days a year. Today was not one of them. It was pissing down.

At least it was early on the walk so spirits were not totally crushed by the rain. In fact we were all in reasonably good form tramping along nicely chatting to the occasional fellow walker and feeling good as the field started to stretch out a bit. The thinning crowd was good as finally it felt that we were actually in the Scottish Highlands and not walking down Oxford Street.

The first part of the walk is a more or less steady pull and reaches a high point after about two and a half hours at some 1050 feet above sea level.

Once we were out of the trees though the weather was decidedly unpleasant with rain blowing into your face. I was already beginning to imagine what Rannoch Moor would be like in this weather and concluded with inescapable logic Fergus would have been proud of, it would be wet.

Onwards we went pretty much as a group at this stage and as the path descended I knew we were approaching Kinlochleven having stayed there a couple of times before. Kinlochleven has a chequered history having been something of a boom town at one point. In the early 1900's the British Aluminium Company embarked on an extremely ambitious engineering project. The first phase built the eight mile long Blackwater Reservoir on top of Rannoch Moor, then the largest in Europe. The reservoir provided hydro electric power used to power a smelting plant in Kinlochleven and this drove a boom time for the area. At its height the plant employed some 800 people. The need for this size of work force fuelled a whole community and houses, schools and churches grew on the back of the aluminium smelter.

The clincher in this booming economy came during World War I. The town still lacked good communication but during WW1 a PoW camp was stationed in the woodlands above Kinlochleven. The PoW's were then gainfully employed in road building and constructed the roads along Loch Leven. I bet nobody bothered to give them midge nets, it must have been a thankless job. A large team of German and Italian road builders could have attracted most of the midge population of Lochaber, I wonder what they made of it all? Before their efforts the access had been primarily by sea.

The improved infrastructure and a burgeoning demand for aluminium saw Kinlochleven enjoy something of a golden age and for the next sixty years or so the village enjoyed a thriving economy.

Sadly but unsurprisingly the smelter eventually closed in 2000 and the village economy now relies mostly on tourism. The WHW is a constant source of weary walkers most pretty hungry and several of our own ilk extremely thirsty.

For the seriously stupid tourist the town also boasts "The Ice Factor" which advertises itself thus:

World's Biggest Indoor Ice Wall, UK's Highest Articulated Rock Climbing Wall

I've always been slightly drawn to the idea of ice climbing. It has an appealing simplicity. Strap some spikes to your boots (techy climbing types would call them crampons) grab a couple of ice axes and walk up the ice. Alternate swings of spiked boot and hand held axe provide the "grip" needed to ascend pretty near vertical ice. On the other hand at 19 stone plus maybe it wouldn't be quite as easy as it looks. When I get down to the 13 stone recommended by recent medical I'll be in better shape to give it a try.

We got slightly separated walking down to the first rest area and several attempts were made to contact each other and John by mobile. These were largely wasted efforts as there was no signal and although John's phone worked fine most of ours were dead having been drowned for four hours on the walk from Fort William.

Also of concern was that my boots had started leaking more or less at the start and I now had very wet feet. These boots proved to be a really bad decision. I knew I needed new boots, my old ones having expired of life but I also was facing a bit of a cash crisis. The usual round of annual reorganisation that seems to be endemic within American high technology companies had left my position "under review" for some time. Never was the phrase "Constant change creates the illusion of progress" better applied than to high technology companies, especially North American ones. If you don't have experience of this industry read "Dilbert" cartoons and you'll learn all you need to know about how North American high tech operates.

Anyway it was during this period of review that I had to buy new boots. Since my position seemed tenuous at best I was extremely concerned about short term cash flow. Rather than spending the needed 100 pounds or so to buy a serious quality pair of boots, I had invested less than 30 in a pair of Decathlon own brand boots in a clear out sale. They claimed they were gortex. They claimed to be three season boots, I was sure they would be fine. Clearly Scotland in summer was part of the fourth season they were not intended for because for 3 hours 52 minutes of the last four hours they had leaked profusely.

After more phaffing around (not John's fault this time) we eventually found him parked up and embarked on a healthy "wolf down" approach to fried egg rolls. They were the

dog's coohanas, really the best fried egg rolls I have ever eaten, or for that matter am ever likely to eat in the future. Spirits were good all round. Socks were changed, it had nearly stopped raining and we had completed 12 miles at an even 3 miles an hour without feeling like we were racing. The only down side was that most (actually, all if memory serves me well) of the walking team mobiles were now dead and my feet were a bit damp. What's a couple of damp feet between friends anyway no problem at all I thought. Leg one then had gone as well as we could possibly hope, leg 2 was the steepest and hilliest leg of the walk, after that it would all be plain sailing. Honest.

The Second Leg Kinlochleven to Glencoe Ski Centre.

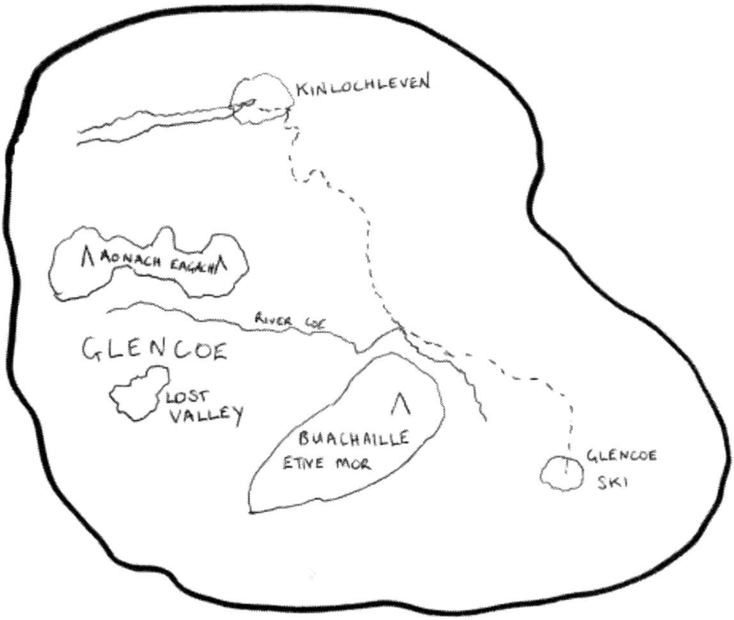

Fortified by the healthy combination of two fried egg rolls, much HP sauce (divide the entire world in two HP sauce vs. ketchup you get an exact split) tea, lucozade sport, raisins, oat cakes and fresh socks we set off in fine spirits. The next leg is the shortest of the walk, only eight miles from Kinlochleven to the Glencoe ski centre but it does reach the high point of the day and has the most uphill grunt.
The high point comes at the top of the Devil's stair case above Glencoe and we were all hoping for a weather

improvement as it should be the best view of the day. Well I guess Loch Lomond might rival Glencoe but if and when we reached Loch Lomond I strongly suspected everyone would be too knackered to care about the view.
At least now it had stopped raining and we could pack away the rain gear for now, just as well as it is a pretty long drag out of Kinlochleven and wearing wet weather gear whilst puffing away uphill tends to result in profuse sweating, especially for fat people amongst whom myself and Mr Martin could count ourselves.
In fact as we pulled up hill from Kinlochleven it was genuine T-shirt weather and turning into rather a nice day. It never ceases to amaze me how fast the weather can change in Scotland you can have four seasons in one hour never mind in one day, and that's only sitting inside the pub.
Inwardly as we pulled up the hill I was beginning what could best be described as a very long internal rant. I was now firmly at the back and uphill definitely the slowest of our famous five. My internal rant followed a consistent theme...

How come Tony and Paul are now faster than me?

I've done just as much if not more training than them?

If I hadn't dragged them out on numerous training walks they would have never even got this far?

Why don't they show some consideration and slow down a bit?

Why is life so unfair and unjust and why am I such a useless fat bastard?

To a very large degree these helpful, positive thinking motivational speeches were conducted entirely with myself and did not extend to articulating any of these thoughts in public. I was also pretty aware that this wasn't going to be a helpful thought process for the next twenty hours or so, but hey sometimes something just gets stuck in your head and you can't avoid it. At least these thoughts weren't "brown girl in the ring".

The walk continues uphill for a further four and a bit miles reaching a high point for the stage and indeed for the entire day at the top of the devil's staircase above Glencoe.

We did actually manage to gather ourselves together at this point for the obligatory group photograph and you could look back and see the footpath meandering into the distance. Walkers were now really strung out and scattered over a considerable distance. Already there were quite some number walking solo and as we chatted amiably to a few adjacent walkers it seems some teams had scattered completely. One poor girl we met had been abandoned completely by her team mates who informing her she was walking too slowly had simply sodded off into the distance with a "see you at the finish, if you make it" sort of message.
Our team had definitely not split and although I continued to get frustrated by my inability to keep up with the pace uphill I felt slightly embarrassed by my internal rants. I resolved to think better of my fine team mates and then knowing Paul's knee was dodgy downhill tried to jog down the Devil's staircase to leave him eating dust. He reciprocated by speeding past me on the flat and then was to be seen jogging several hundred metres with Mark some way ahead. Bastard.

The view from the top of the Devil's staircase did not disappoint. By sheer good fortune this turned out to be the best part of the day and we were rewarded with fine views down Glencoe, across to Buachaille Etive Mor and further round over Rannoch Moor. The down side is that the way across Rannoch Moor left no room for doubt that we were in for a long slog in the next stretch.

Glencoe is a special place. Not only does it possess some of the finest mountain scenery and climbing in Britain it also has a special atmosphere. Everyone who has spent their primary education in Scotland, which includes me, knows the story of treachery that made Glencoe the "Glen of Weeping". In 1691 King William the third decreed that all clan chiefs sign an oath of allegiance by 1st January 1692. Chief of the Macdonald clan MacIain of Glencoe for reasons obscured by the passage of time failed to sign the oath until 6th January. Maybe he was genuinely delayed, more probably it was an act of truculence and defiance that even if coerced he wouldn't completely bow to the would be authority of any English man not even King Billy (well OK I agree he was really Dutch but by this time he was better known to Scots at least as King of England).

King Billy would not suffer this slight quietly. Again the history books don't record his emotions but one can easily imagine that an inner rage burned bright at the snub and in a determined attempt to crush the Jacobite uprising he resolved to teach the Macdonald's a harsh lesson and to send a message to the rest of the clans that any independence, no matter how small, was not going to be tolerated.

The part hard to fathom is that King Billy entrusted this enforcement policy to Campbell of Glenlyon. At least from my upbringing there was only ever one Scottish enemy and that was the English but from the next part of the story on can surmise that the picture was more complex and that Scots sided at times with the English and that at times the conflict between different clans was fierce and violent. Campbell of Glenlyon led a party of some 128 soldiers who travelled to Glencoe and sought safe passage, rest and accommodation from the Macdonald's.

As was long highland tradition, they were it seemed offered complete hospitality and stayed with the Macdonald's for 12 nights. On the 13th February 1692 as the Macdonald's

lay sleeping the Campbell soldiers slaughtered 38 of the Macdonald's with many more dying as they fled to the freezing hills to seek shelter. The night by chance or design was also one of a terrible blizzard (or maybe that is just legend) so any old or infirm who escaped the sword would be sure to perish in the surrounding hills.
The treachery involved in apparent friends accepting hospitality and then turning on their host has given the story its infamy. The slaughter is recorded as being most brutal, the orders given to Glenlyon unequivocal.

To Captain Robert Campbell of Glenlyon

Ballacholis
Feb. 12, 1692
Sir:
You are hereby ordered to fall upon the Rebels, the MacDonalds of Glencoe, and put all to the sword under 70. You are to have especial care, that the Old Fox and his Sons do upon no account escape your Hands, you are to secure all the avenues that no man can escape: this you are to put in Execution at five a Clock in the Morning precisely, and by that time or very shortly after it, I'll strive to be at you with a stronger party. If I do not come at five, you are not to tarry for me but fall on. This is by the King's Special command, for the good and safety of the country, that these miscreants may be cut off root and branch. See that this be put in execution without Feud or Favor, else you may expect to be treated as not true to the King or Government nor a man fit to carry Commission in the King's Service. Expecting you will not fail in the fulfilling hereof as you love yourself, I subscribed these with my hand.

Signed Robert Duncanson
For Their Majesties Service

The story has been one of the most repeated of Scottish history. The "biting the hand that feeds you" aspect is the one that stirs outrage at the Campbells and sympathy for the Macdonalds in equal measure.
Apparently the Clachaig Inn at the bottom of Glencoe used to sport a "No Campbells" sign such was the mistrust of the members of that clan. At least one source I read however claimed that only a small number of Glenlyon's soldiers were actually Campbells. It seems that level of detail is indeed lost to the passage of time and the legend has become the accepted version of events.

Now I don't believe MacIain and I are in any distant way related but I've always thought it poignant that at least in part he was my name sake. In a further Jackson family twist we have had a small family tradition of second Christian names being clan names and my father is James Macdonald Jackson and my brother Alan Campbell Jackson, it is a wonder they get on so well.

Glencoe is actually best approached in my opinion across Rannoch Moor. Rannoch moor is a windswept desolate place, home to midges by the million and constantly raining. As you turn from Rannoch Moor though, and into the head of Glencoe, Buachaille Etive Mor rises from the moor and in instant towers above you and dominates the landscape. It is a magnificent lump of rock. The rock face (which at the top of the Devil's staircase we were now directly facing) faces due south and glistens in any blinks of sunshine. Apparently the rock is predominately "ryolite", whatever the hell that is. All I know about ryolite is that when the sun shines, and especially when the sun shines on wet ryolite, it is exceptionally beautiful.

You can climb the "Buachaille" (pronounced bookle), as it is known to climbers, directly up the main face. The easiest route is by curved ridge, a route my brother describes as "no bother". Then he also told me that the famous Glencoe ridge route the Annoach Eagach was no bother and I know having followed him along it a couple of summers ago that this is a little exaggeration. There is one point you have to step up about a yard onto a ledge about four inches wide with free air all around you and the nearest solid ground a thousand feet below. This I am sure is no bother if you are a regular rock climber climbing E6 grade rock, which from my observations is a 45 degree overhung piece of marble with two tiny blemishes half way up the climber will describe as hand holds that are "bomb proof". If by contrast you are a fat sweaty bloke whose previous experience runs to a few scrambles in the lake District and a short v diff* on a management outward bound course (with a top rope of course) then the exposure on the Annoach is a little bit spooky. I've learnt the hard way not to trust my brother's judgement of routes. It isn't that he deliberately misleads just that he genuinely finds it no bother and finds it difficult to imagine why anyone would find it a struggle.

It's just like the guy at work who says he has played a bit of squash. You turn up for a game which consists of him standing on the T stroking the ball around, not even breaking up a slight perspiration never mind a sweat, whilst you run to all four corners of the court dripping great pools of perspiration onto the court and trying to inhale your

*V Diff = very difficult this translates for real climbers as trivially easy.

lungs that you have inadvertently just regurgitated. Squash is a game where being a bit better than your opponent usually results in a trouncing. Same with climbing, someone who has climbed to a high standard will wander up precipitous rock faces as though going down the shops for a packet of fags. Never listen to someone who tells you curved ridge is "no bother". I still have a hankering to do it but first will seek a sane opinion (i.e. from a novice climber) if it is any more difficult than the Annoach.

I have walked up the Buachaille. There is a hiker's path that goes round the back and really is no bother. You get a great view across Rannoch Moor from the top as far as Schiehallion on a clear day. Without wishing to heap yet more historical context on this part of the tale I have to just mention that Schiehallion was where Newton carried out experiments on gravity, something to do with the symmetrical shape of the mountain I believe. As I said earlier somehow I also made it along the Annoach, despite a few brown trouser moments. My favourite walk in Glencoe is an altogether simpler affair though.

About half way along the glen there is a big car park on the left and a fairly distinct footpath leading up to an obvious watershed. This is the way up to the Lost Valley, for the geologically inclined a fine example of a hanging valley. It is also the location of one of the major rock falls in Scotland where rather than a few frost shattered boulders having formed a small patch of scree a whole side of a hill became detached and some point and now form a magnificent jumble of car sized rocks.

The walk is steep but on a very well made footpath and as long as you ignore the paths to the right and keep to the left where you cross the burn you won't go wrong. If you do stick to the right hand side of the burn you can still

reach the lost valley but it involves a scramble through the rock fall. Any ten year old boys will of course much prefer this way and have a rare old time trying to pick their way through the rock fall.
Once you pop out into the Lost Valley you are rewarded with a place that has a feel of its own. Not visible from the road, in fact hidden from view until the last possible moment, the valley appears by magic and widens out into a grassy flat bottomed meadow. Surrounded on all sides by mountains it is also unusually still and quiet, even on a windy day. Tradition records it is the place the Macdonalds used to hide stolen sheep and cattle after they nicked them from the Campbells, maybe that explains a lot!
No time for the Buachaille, the Annoach or the lost valley today though, after enjoying a short drink and taking in the view we headed down the zig zags that form the Devils staircase and into Glencoe itself.
After such a great view at the bottom there is a short miserable section as the West Highland Way tracks the road closely for a short way and you have to endure traffic noise and fumes for a while. It was the only section of the walk to suffer from this so I suppose about half a mile of traffic intrusion in 54 miles of walking is not too bad.
The path shortly leaves the road and runs parallel to the road for a while without being so close that the traffic is intrusive. The path then turns away from the glen for a while and loops behind the Kingshouse hotel. It must have been the only time in the last six months when we passed a pub vaguely in the vicinity of lunch time that there hadn't been a serious discussion about stopping for a pint. If my memory serves me well no one even mentioned beer.
Paul and Mark had pressed ahead. Tony was next and James was bringing up the rear. The order we perambulated

in could not only reflect fitness but also personality. Mark was way the fittest, James was the next fittest but also the most amicable and team oriented of any of us. Paul was a bit better and faster than me, especially uphill and really competitive. Testing himself was as important to him as racing the rest of us. Tony had improved immensely in fitness but also had an overwhelming objective to keep the team together and above all to be positive and enthusiastic. Me, well I would like to have raced and been in the front, but I couldn't. I was the slowest and so trudged at the back vaguely grumbling to myself and waiting for my chance (never sadly to arrive) to be blessed with a turn of foot that saw me speed to the front.

So distil all that together and you have how we arrived at the next check point at the Glencoe ski lifts.

Mark first, Paul a bit behind, Tony in the middle and James keeping me company at the back for no other reason than he is a thoroughly nice bloke.

John in his self appointed role of team Dad had prepared a feast. A great steaming stew of Heinz big soup had been fortified with additional lentils. On the side were cheese rolls, ham rolls, rolls, biscuits, jaffa cakes and all assorted snacky sundries.

We sat in the sun for a while with the obligatory feet airing and sock changing routine. Everyone except me settled into a large bowl of soupstew. Now here is a conundrum. In the normal run of things I can cheerfully sit down and plough non-stop through 5000 calories of food without hesitation, anything from my Indian take away plus half of Fiona's and the third of Alison's she didn't want, to hoovering so many snacky things at the regulation Xmas buffet that I am closer to the peanut than Jimmy Carter. When I exercise I have trouble to eat. On the few occasions I have walked the Scottish mountains in winter I find it really difficult to get anything down. After a hard game of rugby I couldn't face solids for at least a couple of hours after final whistle (unfortunately at which point I had managed about six pints). Now having walked twenty one miles I wasn't a bit hungry. Soupstew held no appeal at all. I piled branston pickle into a cheese roll and almost literally forced it down it was the best I could do.

I wasn't that bothered, OK this was a longer deal than we had done before but I figured I had enough internally stored calories to fuel 2000 never mind 20 miles.

We started to get our act together, helped on by a couple of chiselled army types wandering round offering encouragement. A few army guys popped up at most check points although I am not sure they had any real purpose other than to look exceedingly fit, they all looked as though they could hop round the whole bloody route in about two hours.

With the improved weather and the next part a long stretch flat and following the route of the old railway I decided to ditch the boots and switch to trainers. I figured they offered more comfort, especially more shock absorbance, and I was hoping it might help me avoid the sole of foot blisters I had been troubled with in training. I also decided at this point it was time for tape and applied a couple of yards of industrial strength zinc oxide tape to my feet. The army strength grade we had picked up at check in the day before.
Suitably fortified we set off but now we were six. The next leg ended at a check point where there was no road access for support so John was going to walk a few miles with us before retracing his steps to pick up the voyageur and drive to checkpoint four. Twenty one miles gone, thirty three to go, optimism high, pace good, blisters none, food on board lots, it would all be plain sailing from here. Simple.

The Third Leg Glencoe Ski Centre to Inveroran (near Bridge of Orchy).

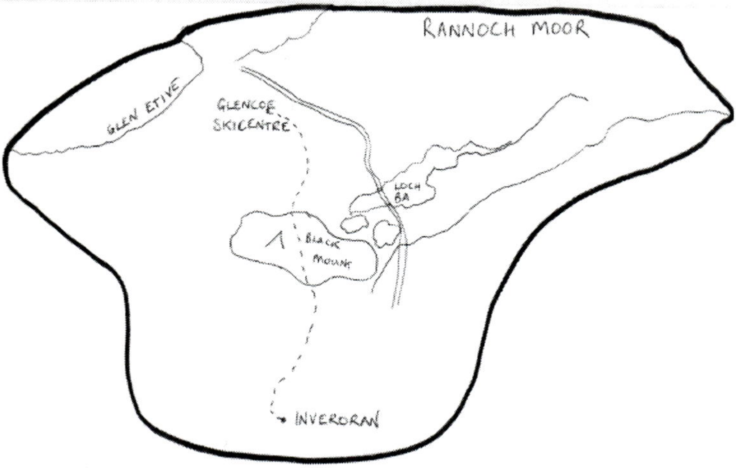

John joining us provided welcome variety to the group. He was fresher than the rest and in good spirits and provided some much needed boosting of the idle banter that kept us going. This was a really nice part of the day now, the sun was shining, if a little weakly, and walking in a T-shirt was perfectly comfortable. The route now winds round Rannoch moor which is a bit of a windswept desolate sort of place. I could hardly recall a time when I'd driven over Rannoch Moor when it hadn't been raining. That wasn't an insignificant number of times. As a child I had summer holidayed in the same part of the Highlands every year and the driving route took us over Rannoch Moor. The Highlands were much less accessible then and the family

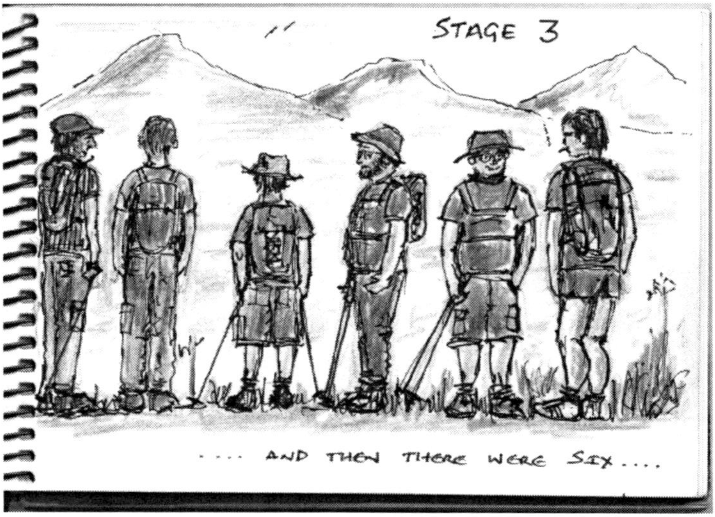

car, a Morris 1000, was loaded to the rafters with clothes and tinned food. By the time the car reached its thirteenth birthday it was suffering somewhat and as you reached the edge of Rannoch Moor two things always happened. It started raining. The queue of cars we collected as we climbed the Black Mount finally had a chance to pass us and were in a rush to do so before being stuck again as the road wound down Glencoe.

Given the conditions at the start I was more than thankful that we were spared horribleness today, it is a really exposed spot and you get awfully wet and cold tramping across Rannoch Moor in bad weather. Robert Louis Stevenson perhaps best sums it up in the novel Kidnapped with this rather bleak but essentially accurate description of the moor *"A wearier looking desert a man never saw".*

Tony by now had not just said hello but chatted for a few minutes to at least 487 of the 695 people that started alongside us. He has endless capacity for seeing the best in humanity and is genuinely interested in what everyone has to say. Unfortunately Tony insisted on sharing his love of mankind with everyone else who as you have gathered by now had just a tad more cynicism than Tony. At one particular moment as I was trudging up a very slight incline Tony was really excited to introduce me to his new best pal. The latest chum Tony had gathered was apparently a buyer or taster or something for one of the distilleries. It might have been Laphroaig but then again it might not. Lovely chap as I'm sure he was, chatting to Tony and him would have meant stopping and losing the hard won five yard gap I had pulled out in front of Tony. I was far more interested in just walking and despite Tony's best efforts to engage me in a conversation I'm afraid I managed little more than a very bad tempered grunt and continued on my way. After all Paul was at least a further five yards ahead of me and my main, no my only, goal was to catch Paul. Why could I possibly want to stop and talk to this bloke even if he was going to offer to sell us an illicit barrel of Laphroaig for four pence?

If it hadn't been such a nice day now this would have been not the most exciting part of the walk. The scenery doesn't change much and there isn't a lot of up and down. Actually those two things do go hand in hand. The reason hill walking is worth the effort is that in no time at all you can look back and think "Crikey did I really start down there". It still surprises me how fast the scenery changes at even my ploddy up hill pace.

We of course weren't the first people to tramp this route. The West Highland Way was opened in 1980 but the origins of the part we were currently tramping go back much further.

The English had for a long time tried to tame the Scots. Some would say they are still trying and some that they never will but let's not go there. The numerous attempts to rule Scotland from Westminster remained only partially successful through many centuries. The particularly troublesome thorn in the English side was the many highland clans that still retained Jacobite sympathies and were prepared to call to arms in support of a Jacobite uprising. Sounds familiar doesn't it, the horrible massacre in Glencoe described earlier stemmed from an attempt to crush loyalties to the house of Stewart but even in the early seventeen hundreds there remained substantial Jacobite support in the highlands.

In a bid to finally wrest control one General Wade was dispatched to the highlands in 1724 for what modern parlance would now describe as a "strategic review" of the effectiveness of the rule of Westminster in these Northern lands. His observations were two fold:

1. There are still a lot of wild Jacobite highlanders armed to the teeth and ready for trouble.
2. Without any roads and few bridges moving an army around fast enough to squash trouble was impossible.

Wade's review was well received and he was appointed commander in chief Northern Britain and in this capacity set about a road building program of ambitious proportions. In all Wade built roughly 300 miles of military roads, all by hand of course. Not as arrow straight as the Roman efforts but none the less there had been nothing on this scale since Roman times. The road we were now following was not in fact Wade's but his successor Caufield who built a further 800 miles of military road around Scotland. A truly astonishing achievement given the lack of mechanisation,

the awful terrain, and the weather Caufield had to contend with.
The impact of the roads is less clear. Highlanders saw them as invasive, hostile and irrelevant. After all they were completely used to travelling the terrain on foot and had no benefit from the roads. The only benefit was to hostile outsiders who had neither the skills nor knowledge to navigate highland terrain without roads.
Now of course the roads are extensively used as public footpaths and provided us with a relatively easy passage. At least in current conditions (daylight, no fog) it was pretty difficult to get lost.
In due course John decided for turning round, he had walked well and seemed not in any special trouble from his calf although there was one hell of a difference between 5 miles and 54 miles. We meandered on mostly in silence occasionally sparking up some new topic for conversation and by the simple expedient of putting one foot in front of

the other enough times we arrived at check point three. Check point three is the veritable zenith of CC check points. With no road access for support drivers the good people organising and volunteering to run the cally challenge had laid on a choice of marvellous things to do. The range of possibilities were quite enticing, one could get feet repaired by the nice St John's ambulance people, one could eat the free food on offer, one could listen to the band bashing out "If I could walk five hundred miles" or one could get a free massage. A quick survey of what was on offer led to some pretty crystal clear decisions.

Choice 1: If I join the queue now I get to be next in line for a massage from the extremely pretty (as it turned out) Irish physio lady who (also as it turned out) will turn my weary legs into fully functional positively energised limbs of steel.

Choice 2: I can listen to this god awful band play "If I could walk five hundred miles" for at least the fourth time since my arrival ten minutes ago in which case if I had a gun the lead singer would not be long for this world.

I settled for massage first and feet repair second. Foot repair was starting to be a concern. I had some pretty meaty heel blisters and first signs of hot spots on the sole of my foot. The nice man from the St John's drained and patched the heel blisters but not too much he could do about the sole of feet trouble. He also looked at me somewhat quizzically and asked if was going to carry on which I returned with an equally puzzled countenance as I had not the slightest idea that anything at this level of foot trouble would lead to a nanosecond of contemplation about stopping. Once St John's had finished though, I took the added precaution of wrapping several yards of the essential industrial strength zinc oxide tape around the sore parts.

Food was less of a satisfying experience. I was by now

getting hungry again having gone through my unable to eat phase and chilli with rice hit the spot pretty well. The only trouble was the portion size was roughly a thimble full and as I sat down I breathed deeply and accidently inhaled the whole plateful in one go.

I later learned Tony had gone round three times with no problem which begs the question why they didn't just give you three times as much in the first place. If you do this challenge at any time in your life take extra food with you between CP2 and CP4. Having failed to twig the "go back for second helpings" approach, I was now in serious calorie debt territory with a long way to CP 4 and only a few chewy bars for sustenance.

All of us had gone for massage therapy although I got a lot of stick for securing the pretty Irish lady when the others got blokes older than ourselves. Tony had also had running foot repair although his feet didn't look in too bad shape. Mark had smoked several roll ups. Fed, massaged, smoked and watered we gathered together and made our way out the main tent to start stage four. Paul had gone missing though and cries of "Paul?" were met with a muffled response from inside the nearest portaloo.

What seemed like an age later Paul emerged grinning followed closely by a Chernobyl sized gas cloud that had us beetling up the road at high speed. The portaloo now carried a health warning because anyone entering it without wearing a WW1 gas mask was going to be in big trouble. I considered it tantamount to cheating. He must be at least a stone lighter now was my somewhat uncharitable thought.

So we were off, thirty two miles gone, twenty two to go, food on board not enough, blisters some, pace still good, optimism medium. Nothing could go wrong.

Charity

As we were now starting to become aware that this challenge was not a walk in the park I'd like to say that we fell back on the deep satisfaction of all of this being for charity. I'd like to say that but can't. The naked truth is that the charity component of the whole enterprise was mostly viewed by the whisky club as a pain in the arse. Not that the charity receiving our funds wasn't a highly laudable one. The Scottish Community Foundation does excellent work filling a role not covered by bigger organisations.
A quick browse on their web pages finds a whole host of worthy causes funded by the SCF. A completely random and pointless cut and paste from the web site provided a list of small worthy causes who one assumes would find it very difficult to generate funds elsewhere.

Rag Tag N Textile Collective, Highland: £47,147.50*

Sikh Sanjog, Edinburgh City: £50,506*

Connecting Generations

Helmsdale Heritage Society, Highland: £48,167.10*

Radio Fyneside, Argyll & Bute: £49,962

It has to be said though our motivation was all about the physical challenge but we had signed up to raise 500 pounds each and that we would do.
The obvious tactic in these cases is to ask your mates to sponsor you. At five quid a person though that would be a hundred people, and even if you know a hundred people prepared to donate a fiver each it was still going to be an exercise akin to painting the Forth Road Bridge to get them

to sign the sponsor form and then go back and collect the money later.

I decided out of pure laziness to go for targeting any of my friends likely to donate at least twenty quid. Some would donate more so if could get the ADPU (Average Donation Per User) up to at least thirty quid I only needed 16.666 donations to break the five hundred quid target. Also out of pure laziness I opted to target people who were prepared to donate directly on to the cally challenge web site. There is actually a small real benefit here in that as long as the donatee is a UK tax payer the tax man will also make an in kind contribution. Amen to that I say squeezing money out of the tax office is right up there with drinking whisky and watching rugby union as amongst the better things to do with ones time.

Of course the preferred mode of asking was also extremely efficient (or lazy if you prefer). Send the right tone of email to the thirty or so identified candidate donatees and sit back and wait for my cally challenge account to fill up with five hundred of the finest British pounds. My effort at this one shot wonder approach went as follows:

From: Iain Jackson
Sent: 13 February 2006 18:42
To: Iain Jackson
Subject: Sponsorship Plea

All,
Out of some kind of middle aged madness myself and my good chums from the Gravesend Windmill Hill Scottish Malt Whisky Society have entered the Caledonian Challenge. (http://www.caledonianchallenge.com/) This is a tough challenge. 54 miles of the West Highland Way to be completed in 24 hours. Since you all know me

well you'll be pretty sure I'll give it my all to finish it, here are a few reasons it will be tough:

54 miles is a long way
24 hours is a long time without a drink (alcohol variety)
I weigh in as you know at well North of 18 stone
For some substantial part of the day it will be raining (it is Scotland after all)
Midges
Blisters

So go on to the sponsor a team link on their web site and look for The Gravesend Malt Whisky Club. Any donation will be helping all kinds of small Scottish charities from a day care center on the island of Lewis to a project recycling carpet for homeless people who have just been homed in Glasgow.
If nothing else you can also inwardly smile at the pain and suffering I'll be going through on the 16th June

Cheers
Jacko

Iain Jackson
Engineering

I thought I had captured the balance between my suffering and their potential generosity pretty well. It was the third go though on the first two I had written an Ellen

MacArthuresque description of the challenge as really really tough or very very demanding. UGH! If I have done that in this book feel free to send me thousands of abusive emails. Have you ever read an Ellen MacArthur book? I tried to read her account of breaking the single handed round the world record "Race Against Time". Don't get me wrong the achievement is without parallel and I can only stand amongst the crowd in amazement and marvel at her efforts. But the book...by day seventeen of her seventy one and a bit day journey you have passed 11 events that were "very very" something, one that was "really really" something else and on two further occasions it was all "much much" too something. I know it was tough but surely English has some alternatives to allow a description of events that convey more to the reader than repeating yourself quite so often. Sorry Ellen I'm not in full command of the language either but the last much much was too much for me and I never got past day seventeen.

Plaudits to the team scribing the back cover though I'd sign them up tomorrow for any future publication. The "it's not what you say it's what you don't say approach" raised a chuckle with me, it was absolutely tip top marketing. I would have been proud of it.

The reported crits go as follows:

"The single greatest sporting feat of the year.... In any sport. In any nation" *Sunday Express*
"MacArthur embarked on this journey as a yachtswoman and returned as a symbol of human aspiration" *Daily Telegraph*

“MacArthur is wonderful, fabulous, inspiring. She is a bringer of joy and an emblem of hope” *The Times*

Agreed. But these are crits of the achievement not of the book. The singular lack of mention of the MacArthur prose is very very revealing.

My email one shot wonder approach was not exactly bringing home the bacon but it was at least partially effective. Everyone had adopted slightly different strategies. Tony was embarrassing his customers into donating large sums, James was steadily collecting a veritable mountain of commitments, Mark was off on the Forth Road bridge strategy by collecting five hundred one pound pledges from teaching colleagues and fellow footballers and John had adopted the do sod all and wait till later approach. Lucky for him he didn’t eventually walk or collecting five hundred quid in the last two weeks before the event might have proved difficult.

I decide to embark on a one man campaign to speed up the whole fund raising process. The campaign was clearly managed and orchestrated by Fergus since the sum total of my effort was to raise an additional zero pounds and zero pence.

This totally futile exercise involved three parallel approaches.

My first idea was to write a series of articles and have them published in a walking magazine following our training and then reporting on the walk itself. Each article would end with the web link to the Cally Challenge sponsorship page and would without question fill our coffers rapidly. Great idea but having written the first article I couldn’t think of what to do with it and it actually became the seed that eventually became this book instead.

Second I wrote to every whisky distillery I could think of begging sponsorship. It wasn't a totally "give me money" plea I promised them two things:

1. They would have exclusive rights to use the GWHSMWS and its achievements in completing the Caledonian Challenge in a worldwide advertising campaign sure to double their revenue stream.
2. I was going to write a book based on the experience which would become extremely famous and provide them with free advertising for years to come.

Of course they declined the first value proposition and didn't believe the second, cynics. We voted at whisky club in reciprocation not to buy Laphroaig, Glenmorangie, Glenfiddich, or Glenlivet for a while as they had all sent us standard reply letter A which loosely translated told us to go and find alternative sources for sponsorship as they already donated vast fortunes to multiple charities.

The third genius idea was an extension of a plan carefully crafted on our long training walk. Baldrick couldn't have done better. Jools Holland is local, he's got pots of money we'll write to him and ask him for some.

This time I nailed it and I pitched four perfect reasons it was a good idea for him to sponsor us.

1. We were living locally
2. We had walked past his house many times whilst training.

3. His wife is Scottish and this was all for Scottish charity (not even sure if this is true it was a throw away comment from a fat bloke in the pub).
4. He has got pots of money so can clearly spare some to sponsor us

It wasn't to be honest that much of a surprise when I received standard letter B telling us politely to seek our sponsorship fortunes elsewhere. At least he actually signed it himself and the whisky club decided that having been very polite and good enough to sign it we would refrain from an extended boycott of his future concerts. I am sure Jools took due account of our fair mindedness and was delighted to continue to enjoy our patronage, or more probably he didn't even notice.

Well although my significantly over achieve strategy to garner thousands from the whisky industry and local celebrities (all right celebrity if you want be pedantic about it) constituted abject failure, my personal sponsorship campaign was having better success. Thanks to huge generosity from my friends the jeweller, the yen broker, the IT general manager and the EDA head honcho, four donations had got me over 50% of my target. With only a modicum of chasing down and annoying emails to other friends I reached my 500 pound sponsorship goal relatively painlessly.

Everyone else by hook or by crook also made it, James excelled and nearly raised double his target and at the end of it all we had comfortably exceeded our two and a half grand goal for the team. Now all that was left was to finish the bloody walk.

Stage four Inveroran to Auchtertyre Farm

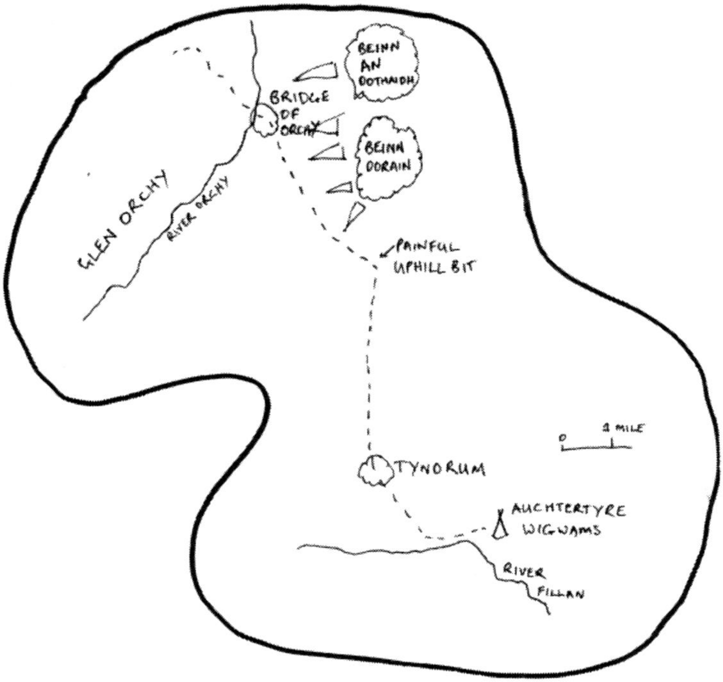

As we left checkpoint three I actually felt pretty good. In fact team spirits were reasonably high. For sure the massage had helped a lot it, really did feel for a while that you were walking on air. I occasionally get the same feeling when running or hiking when maximum effort is sustained for a long period and then the effort slackens slightly but you don't have to stop. If you're slogging on a long uphill trudge in the mountains then crest the ridge and keep going (stopping ruins the effect) then the next twenty minutes on the ridge feel fantastic. I'm not sure of the physiology but my completely uninformed guess is that your muscles recover much faster than the blood supply slows down. Maybe then the heart keeps pumping extra blood into the muscles for a while after it is actually needed, hence the feeling of rejuvenation. One can easily imagine a massage to tired muscles having the same new blood replenishment rejuvenation mechanism.

Of course this reasoning is based on the sound scientific principle of guess work so it could equally well be complete rubbish.

Whatever the reason stage four wasn't going to let us get carried away with ourselves. All of two hundred yards after leaving the checkpoint the path turns once more uphill. Two further hundred yards later and I was at the back. Again. Mark being a complete racing snake was off, Paul chasing him, Tony next and James as before keeping me company. This time I did grumble a bit to James about my inconsiderate team members, it was really just recreational grumbling though. It was now around 8pm and we had been going since 7am and had been up since 5am and despite flashes of feeling good we were all fairly obviously pretty tired.

Although by far not the biggest climb of the day a subsequent review of the route dug out the information that we had ascended to a height of 1075 feet above sea level and that we had walked uphill for a mile. Boy did that seem like a long mile. At this stage at least the weather was still quite pleasant and following the ascent we regrouped (i.e. everyone waited for me) and began a long rather boring slog. The route now runs parallel to the railway that runs from Glasgow Queen Street to Fort William and on to Mallaig.

I have travelled it a couple of times and although I can't compare with other famous railway journeys, in my estimation it is certainly one worth making, especially if you are lucky enough to complete it on a day when the clouds take it upon themselves to rise above three thousand feet and you can see the views.
Although from a completely different part of Scottish history, there are some parallels between the railway and the military road we were still hoofing along. Well over a hundred and fifty years after General Wade recommended his road building scheme the West Highland railway building was started in 1889. Like the road building I really struggle to come to terms with the engineering achievement of building communication systems across this terrain. Apparently the railway was one of the first major constructions to make extensive use of concrete which features in the many bridges and tunnels need to cross stream and hollow out hill sides. More incredible still is that to get the railway across the substantial bog that is Rannoch Moor the railway was literally floated on top of the bog. I am not sure if this is completely true or not (and I totally accept that a facet of internet research is that occasionally you turn up facts too unbelievable to be true largely because they are complete crap) but the solution to the Rannoch Moor bog was to float the railway on a "cork" made of brushwood, tree roots, earth and ashes. If it is true, or even partially true then it is not just the engineering feat that is remarkable but the notion that someone somewhere sat in an office and said I know how to get the line across Rannoch Moor, "We'll float it!".
By 1901 the railway was extended all the way to Mallaig and if you do ever make the trip I'd thoroughly recommend not stopping at Fort William but going all the way to

Mallaig. The scenery will repay the effort. I'd especially suggest going in the late summer or autumn when the heather in bloom can turn the hillside vibrant shades of blues and purple.

Mallaig now is mostly a gate way for ferries to Skye and other parts of the Hebrides. The original intent of the railway though was fish, more specifically herring. Tons and tons of herring were landed in Mallaig and speedily shipped South by rail. Mallaig to Fort William in 1900 would have taken a whole day by rough hill track and mail coach. In 1901 after the railway opened it took less than two hours. On top of course you can fit a hell of a lot more herring in a train truck than you can in a mail coach.

It never ceases to amaze me how we have plundered our seas. From the early 1900's the herring industry in Mallaig grew, slowly for a long time but as increasingly sophisticated fishing methods arrived herring catches boomed in the 1960's. By the 1970's stocks had dwindled so alarmingly that a total ban on herring fishing was imposed for four years. Today it seems as if we have learnt absolutely nothing and cod stocks are heading the same way.

Even in my own little angling world and very short lifetime I have seen dramatic changes in our seas. I can think of a spot in Ardnamurachan where as a kid we would never fail to catch flounder and plaice. It is now completely barren on a very good day you might extract a dogfish. On Loch Ewe on a memorable childhood evening from 1971 we filled a fish box with haddock and cod from the bench seats of a tiny rowing boat. On the same trip I hooked and landed what my Dad clearly thought was a piece of giant seaweed but actually turned out to be a thornback ray. To a ten year old boy this was as exciting as if I'd landed a killer whale so strange and huge did the fish seem. In the same spot now you might feather a few mackerel if they are there, and if they are not you might manage a ten ounce pollock. Someone in government needs to wake up before our seas are empty. I am no great fan of protectionism as a sustainable economic paradigm but still it seems the only people with a solid fishing industry and good fish stocks are the Icelanders. Enough said.

A train actually passed as we were grunting along and with no discernible gradient we were in a reasonably tight bunch for once. I am not sure this was a good thing. At this point Paul announced he was suffering from bad nipple chaffage. Even worse than that, he offered to let Dickins repair the damage. Now I don't know about you but I wouldn't choose a man who feels no pain as my Florence Nightingale for any part of my anatomy, much less a

sensitive area, even less than that sore nipples. Mark found the ideal solution. Two strips of gaffer tape and problem solved........for now. Good luck Paul on detaching that tape later I mused, that is going to hurt. Still that was for later for now it did the job perfectly and Paul was restored to full working order.
Shortly after that the path turned hard left and went under the railway line and then started another uphill meander. Ten strides of uphill and we were all collectively wishing for a bit more boring slog. This was now getting to be hard work. Every uphill step was slow and hard. I can't vouch for the others but at least I knew all about it in my quads. Neither of the ascents on this leg had registered in pre walk reviews of the route, only post pain map studying revealed this second climb to also ascend over 1000 feet and climb uphill steadily for over a mile and a half. Lurking in my mind at this point was that although these ascents hadn't registered, the one after check point four through the Ciranlarich forest had featured in pre walk discussions and along with the ascent to the top of the Devil's Staircase we had tipped it as one of the tougher parts of the route. The inevitable conclusion of this line of reasoning was that we still had the hardest bit to go and to say I wasn't looking forward to that would have been a mild understatement.
Eventually we crested the summit and descended for a bit to the outskirts of Tyndrum. I was slightly perplexed to find an intermediate checkpoint here since in my mind we must have been nearly at checkpoint four. I none the less grabbed a cup of soup (it was horrible by the way) and chatted amiably to the helpers dishing out soup and lucozade sport. Unfortunately for me they cheerfully informed me that we had "*only*" 4 miles to go to checkpoint four. I was crestfallen. In terms of effort and time I was sure we were

nearly at checkpoint four. I was equally sure I had checked the map a while ago and Tyndrum was just round the corner from the Auchtertyre wigwams. Wrong. To boot it was now raining again. I wasn't feeling my best.

It really was a pity that I suffered a trough at this particular point as the walk from Tyndrum to Aucthertyre should have been one of the high points. The West Highland Way follows the course of the first a small tributary and the main River Fillan for almost the whole way between Tyndrum and Aucthertyre.

Although now around 11pm it was only just dusk and clouds of insects hovered above the stream and almost glimmered in the last vestiges of daylight. In any other circumstance I would have pictured myself casting a fly onto the river expectant at any moment for a take from a wild brown trout. To have simply stopped and stared at such a beautiful scene would have been enough to make a man truly happy. I was not happy. I was downright fed up. I trudged along feeling very low, the surrounding tranquillity and beauty utterly lost on me.

Of course we did eventually arrive at checkpoint four and after the huge success of massage at CP3 we immediately joined the massage queue. As soon as I lay down I knew I was cold. One minute later I was in some trouble. I started shivering pretty badly. Since the intermediate checkpoint I had carried on walking in a T-shirt but it had got dark and it was drizzling all the way. I hadn't felt cold walking but I was damn cold now. I left my massage found John and sat down. Now I was shaking pretty badly and my teeth were chattering as well. I don't normally feel the cold as bad as others but when I do get cold I take ages to warm up. Walking in a wet T-shirt combined with too little food had caused temporary system melt down.

As I was looking back on the whole story I found my email advice to everyone written just after finishing the 37 miler, noted below for future entrants in the Cally Challenge to read and perhaps even digest.

Sent: 2 May 2006
To: Iain Jackson; Paul Martin; James Pilcher; John Milner; Tony Kennedy; Mark Dickins
Subject: Re: Saturday

We completed 37.1 miles in 13 hours 45 minutes. Including Cooling Church, map reading and blister repair I estimate we stopped for about an hour in total giving us a ground speed of almost exactly 3 miles an hour. I have some nasty blisters but otherwise fine, how is everyone else?

While I remember I have some key lessons learnt to share.

- Drink more I was seriously dehydrated. A camelbak is a must for me stopping to get my drink bottle out of my bag is not going to happen.
- Repair blisters as soon as you first feel them. I ignored mine which I noticed about Cliffe Fort because I couldn't be bothered to deal with them so close to home. It has probably cost me two days of recovery before I can run again.
- I have to figure a better eating strategy. I roughly counted my calories and reckon I ate less than 2000 calories but burnt closer to 10 000, not sure how to deal with this yet.
- Trainers are a must for me (as long as it is not pissing down) between CP2 and CP4 on the actual event. We'll go over the terrain for each stage Wednesday.
- Watch body temperature as it gets to evening. I was seriously cold as soon as I stopped having been wearing

only a sweaty T-shirt all the way round. This could have been serious if there had been another 17 night time miles to go. Again this was being a bit lazy as I was "close" to the finish.

- Don't start too fast especially as the first bit is up a long drag on the real event. I will be quite happy if we are last into CP1 and CP2 it will set up us much better for the rest of the event.

Overall I think it was a really positive tick in the box. We did 68% of the miles and about 50% of the ascent of the real event and had used 57% of the time. We had 10 hours left to do the last 17 miles and on the real event we won't be carrying packs. On top of that I don't intend to prepare the evening before by drinking a bottle of red wine and getting four and a half hours sleep!!!
See you Wednesday 8:30 chez Jackson.
Iain

It really was a damn shame I hadn't followed any of my own advice. I felt completely shit.
I am convinced there is something wrong with my temperature control mechanism. I have even been to the Doctors and had my temperature measured and failed to register on the thermometer as my body temperature was too low to push the mercury over the little bump needed to create a reading.
I've always had the opinion this must be a contributing factor to me being such a fat bastard, so if there are any physiologists or nutritional scientists studying for a PhD on the relationship between natural body temperature,

metabolic rate, and body fat concentration I'm your man. Lucky for me I had a personal assistant to get me out of my slump. John at this point was a Godsend. Looking back I am pretty sure without someone as focused on what to do I would have given up. No time for discussion he made a trip to the car to get clean dry clothes, then another trip for extra layers, then another trip for chocolate cake and munchies then he sat down and insisted I eat.

I contemplated my options. At one point I even discussed with James if I should seek help from the medics but I knew this was a cop out. If I turned up at the medical centre looking ghostly white and shaking with cold they would probably tell me to stop. How much easier to give up if someone tells you to do it? It wouldn't have been my fault then professional advice could have been cited as the single reason for stopping. It wouldn't at all have been me having the back bone of a jelly fish and throwing the towel in. I decided against the medical centre and settled for waiting a bit more instead.

Up to now we had stuck to our twenty minutes per check point rule, now we were half an hour in and hadn't got ourselves together at all. I started to feel at least a bit human and after John insisted I put on dry clothes and an extra fleece I stopped shivering. Much chocolate cake and hot soup were also downed and I felt I could go on. One more important point to tend before moving on and I hauled my socks off to change them. I figured I need some of my zinc tape updated. In particular I had a sore spot on the bottom of my foot and wanted fresh tape on it to protect it. I was sat down and John (now reaching hero proportions in the helping out stakes) had my foot on his thigh and peeled bag the offending zinc tape. A small puddle of ooze descended on his leg. I looked down and observed that the zinc tape had come off but so had a very large piece of my skin from the top of my foot. One of the omnipresent army guys (Scottish variety) appeared from nowhere and in a blinding moment of perspicacity observed "That disnae look so good". I had to agree with him.

We agreed on a sensible course of action John hurriedly replaced the tape/skin combo he had removed and plastered several miles more tape on top. The walking in soaking wet boots for the first stage had come home to roost in spades. I have pretty soft skin any way but having soaking wet feet had made it worse. Taping on top had only exacerbated the problem and now had a patch of very sore foot with a tape/tape glue/skin layer to add to the considerable blister collection I had assembled.

John (now in the saintly category of helpers) fetched my boots from the car since I could do with extra sock layers and not least because it was now pissing down. Again. Well it is Scotland after all.

So that was it. We had wasted a full hour, forty minutes

more than target turnaround time. I was so wrapped up in my own travails I have no idea how the rest of the team passed that hour, waiting for me mostly I suppose. A final recommendation from John to wear extra layers and a share out of chocolate bars to stuff into pockets and we were ready for the off, John would walk the first mile with us, unsaid but assumed that if I couldn't carry on he would walk back to the checkpoint with me.
As we went to leave I looked around for the first time proper at checkpoint four to survey a scene straight out of M.A.S.H. There were half dead bodies everywhere frantically taping feet or passing out in corners, Christ almighty whose idea was this?
The only comforting point was we were not under time stress. A steady pace and short check point stops early on left us well ahead of the clock. As we left the checkpoint it was 1 am. Six hours to finish within 24 hours. 42 miles gone. 12 to go. Food on board limited to a variety of chocolate based products. Blisters on blisters with added blisters. Optimism reduced to Tony. Would we actually finish this thing?

Stage Five Auchtertyre to Ardleish (the finish)

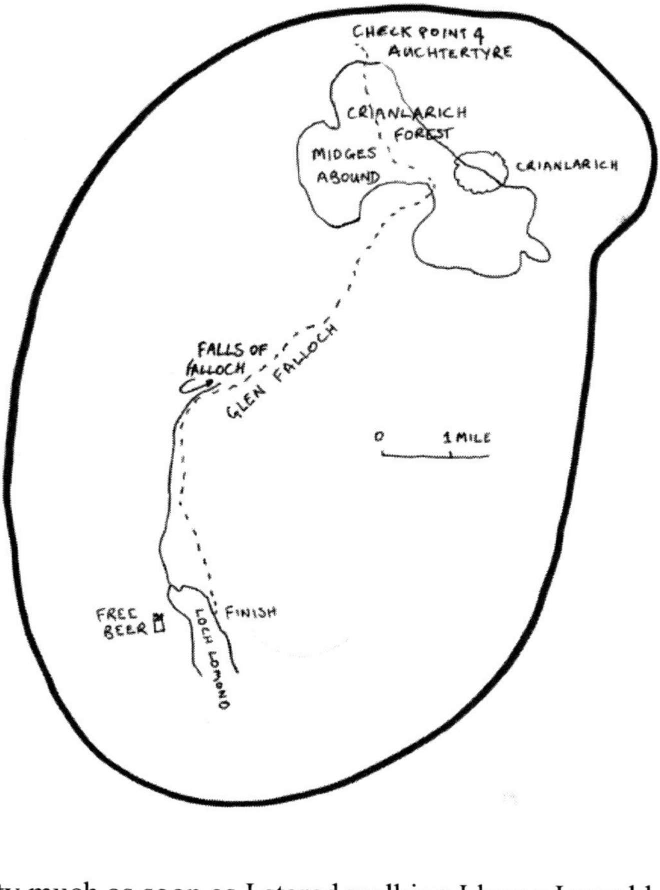

Pretty much as soon as I stared walking I knew I would be OK. I had recovered from my temporary temperature collapse and felt tired but not completely shit. There had been five minutes after I stopped my massage when I felt really bad, but it had been fleeting and I was OK.

My feet were a bit sore but not painful. It is sometimes hard to remember pain the mind will store away that something hurt but not how much. I did have some frames of reference though. On my 0-10 pain scale I mentally rated a few events.

Normal life 0
Nettle rash 1
Blisters and missing skin as identified at checkpoint four 2
A good shoeing whilst lying offside at bottom of a ruck (deserved rugby injury) 3
Whisky Club hangovers 4
Shingles 5
Torn intercostals muscles (rugby injury) 6
Broken collar bone (rugby injury) 7
Herniated disc (rugby injury) 8.

Anything justifying an 8 on a pain scale needs a little more explanation. A small description of a herniated disc is needed to visualise why it hurts so much. A disc in your back is pretty much like a round of wood cut from a tree. It is a series of concentric rings but unlike a tree the middle is a jelly like substance not solid (probably to give a disc its shock absorbing qualities). When you herniate your disc a radial crack develops in the disc and the jelly like substance creeps out and if you are unlucky the resulting bulge presses directly on a nerve. In my case I've done my L4-L5 disc twice which means the nerve it is pressing on is in the lower leg and you get a toothache like pain in the shin. Worst of all if you sit down for any length of time the pressure on the disc (at its maximum when sitting) causes extra fluid to seep and when you stand up again the pressure on the nerve increases. In my case I have

an extremely vivid and unpleasant memory of driving to Sidmouth on a family holiday when recovering from my first bout of disc trouble. When I got out of the car after three hours driving I was very nearly sick on the pavement as an excruciating pain appeared in the front of my left shin. The pain level was not fun.
Of course these are only my personal references as it isn't really feasible to get inside someone else's head and compare notes on how you feel their pain. I am also equally sure there much worse things in life than a herniated disc so I've left 9 & 10 on this scale for really improbably nasty happenings I hopefully don't encounter on the rest of my life journey.

So my current foot state rated only a two, a bit worse than nettle rash but not as bad as a whole host of other eminently survivable conditions. I reckoned that the first condition on my list that might have stopped me walking was shingles at around five and the first that would certainly have stopped me walking was the torn intercostal muscles at six. I had plenty of room to deteriorate and still keep going.
John obviously reached the same conclusion fairly quickly as after about half a mile he turned round and headed back to CP4 to drive onto CP5 and hopefully grab a few hours' kip.

I knew we would now finish, barring some new disaster descending on us, but I also knew the next four or five hours would not consist of fun. As predicted from our previous map studies the path starts to ascend again as soon as you cross the main road at Crianlarich and ascends pretty steeply up through the forest. It was now drizzling steadily, it was two am and from somewhere the midges had come out in force. It was all I could do to plod up the hill and

I was now seriously slowing down the rest of our party. Tony in a frenzy of midge frustration and being completely knackered shot off up the slope. His claim when we caught him up twenty minutes later was that if he continued to walk slowly he would have ground to a complete stop. I couldn't say I blamed him I was really slow and stopping fairly regularly to rest and as soon as you stopped the midges were insufferable. Now much has been written and said about the Scottish midge but I couldn't in all honesty complete any tale of highland adventure without a segway to the midge.

Culicodes Impunctatus the highland midge is the main culprit, to be precise the female of the species as the females are the only ones that bite. If you have not been to Scotland they are pretty hard to imagine. Forget the mosquito these are nothing like the mossie. Much smaller they are tiny specks of blackness hard to pick out as any discernible life form. If you are sweating a lot, which I am most of the time, a few hundred midges will drown in your sweat. When you wipe them from your skin you get a collection of black specks of dirt. At that distance they look pretty harmless. The special feature of the midge that makes it such a nuisance is its vast numbers. When at their worst there are thousands if not millions of them surrounding you. I tried to find a figure for midge population density in Scotland. The people who make the marvellously named "midge eater max" claim in places there are fifty million midges per hectare. Now I may have told you earlier that the human perception of number ends at seven but as I trudged through the Ciranlarich forest I guarantee there were fifty million midges camped in my right ear hole. Not nice.

Worse than that, the damn midge has a preference for some over others. From experience I would say the fois gras and champagne of the midge world is a fat sweaty bloke, preferably a blond or red haired variety with soft skin. In other words, me.

Concatenating my personal midge nightmare the female biting midge exudes some kind of scent that signals to other nearby midges that she has found a useful food source. The consequence of all of this is the attractive food source (me) gets an unfair share of the local midge population to dinner, whereas the less attractive food source (Mark) gets away nearly scot free.

There are numerous possible remedies to the midge. Ask any regular hiker, fisherman, or forestry work in Scotland for a midge repellent and you will get a hundred different answers, here are just a few:

Smoke a pipe/cigar preferably a really smelly one
Chain smoke Capstan (unfiltered)
Eat lots of garlic/curry/vitamin B12/marmite
Spread on your skin lavender oil, pituany oil, camphor, wormwood, mugwort, dill, fennel, citronella.........................
Incredibly expensive chemicals from all kinds of manufacturers
Wear undiluted Skin-so-Soft bath oil, produced by Avon Cosmetics
High frequency sound generators that allegedly deter the midge
Cover yourself head to foot in bees wax
Drink a vast amount of whisky, doesn't get rid of the midges you just don't notice them anymore.

Not one of these solutions will offer the midge even the most token deterrent. I am convinced most of them attract extra midges. The only solution to keeping them out of your hair, eyebrows, nose and ears is to wear a midge net. If you don't believe me look at people who work regularly in the forest and see what they do. They will be wearing midge nets when the midges are at their worst. Discussing other possible solutions is simply a way to fill up your time when engaged on twenty four hour hikes and you have exhausted every other possible topic of conversation.

Eventually of course the slope stopped going uphill and joy, we left the forest which introduced to our lives a breath of breeze which in turn gets rid of the midges. A short while after that we reached a check point six miles into the stage. Only six miles left and we still had three and a bit hours in which to do it. This checkpoint, in addition to the usual

volunteers, was also manned by some of the army hard men we had seen floating around other check points.
Here at least they seemed to have definite purpose and were serving up soup. At least it was claimed to be soup. Clearly it started life as some kind of dried cup-a-soup like powder. Despite the cup being topped with incendiary hot water it had retained all of its gritty powder like qualities and had taken on not a single recognisable characteristic of what reasonable people would call soup.
It was a gritty, foul tasting, undrinkably hot liquid and sludge mixture that took an unfeasible leap of imagination to label as soup.
I guessed that although I was hungry and tired neither quality would have registered on the scale needed to define this soup as desirable. Maybe the yomp across the Falklands to Goose Green would have been the benchmark hungry and tired level for this stuff to be palatable.
We threw away the soupsludge, drank some water and carried on our way. Not long to go now nearly over.
I was desperately weary, sort of worn out by the whole thing. It wasn't that I felt physically that bad it just seemed that having walked for so long it took some willpower to put one foot in front of another and keep going. Just right now was the absolute maximum benefit of doing this as a team. There is almost no doubt in my mind that for me at least doing this with my mates increased my probability of finishing tenfold. I know others are different but Reinhold Messner I definitely am not and doing it alone would have been a struggle. Actually doing it as a team was also a struggle but one that we looked like conquering. Another hour of mostly flat walking brought us again to a most picturesque river side, this time with added waterfall. It was even more lost on me than the last heavenly vision of

tranquillity. In fact raising me out of my torpor would have required a landscape featuring the Niagara Falls with a back drop of Everest and the wildlife of the Serengeti streaming past. I was too knackered to care about anything except crossing the bloody finish line.

Shortly after this we reached the penultimate check point. Not much more than a pile of water bottles and a sign telling us we had two and a half miles to go.

We were now on the shores of Loch Lomond and really not caring whether we were taking high road or low road or any bloody road as long as sometime soon we could stop walking. A narrow single track path took us uphill for the last time and as it was narrow I had to stop frequently to let the queue of faster walkers past. It was a bit of a puzzle how come so many people who had also been walking for 22 hours were all so much faster than me. Much later on it dawned on me that those streaming past were the 9am starters finishing in sub twenty hours, no wonder they still had some gas in the tank.

Loch Lomond itself is worth a visit. The nearby Munro Ben Lomond offers some fantastic views of the Loch for a modicum of effort. The best views are achieved fairly quickly, you don't have to get remotely close to climbing the whole mountain. If you are really lucky as you gain height up the path, the early morning mist will sit on the water of the Loch with the many Islands that are a feature of the Loch will stick their heads through the mist. It can be a beautiful and surreal view. Only the sight of Excalibur appearing from the mist is missing for it to be the perfect setting for some Arthurian legend.

Today it was also early morning and it might or might not have been misty. You'll have gathered by now that my main view for the last hours had been of my feet willing them to keep moving so we could get this thing done. At last the finish hove into view along with about two billion bloody midges that had been attracted by all the sweaty walkers huddled in a tent waiting for their boat ride back to the other side of the Loch. The midges were truly appalling on the last few hundred yards but I didn't care we had finished. James and I crossed the line together the last of our five to finish. Mark was there as photographer and Tony was huddled in a heap, a beaming and happy heap though. Paul was nowhere to be seen and had sodded off to the other side of the Loch. So much for the grand plans to finish as a team.

In fairness though as Paul had crossed the finish line the young lady assigning you a boat number had promoted him straight to the front of the queue on the grounds that he looked tired.

Unsurprisingly everyone else in this queue also looked quite tired so to be the stand out candidate for queue jumping he must have been in a bad way. To boot the midges were horrendous.

We just shrugged and didn't think much more about it, although it did provide useful ammunition to goad Paul with for many a long time after as he suffered guilt pangs for not having waited for his team.

Anyway the total time spread for line crossing was Mark Dickins eventual holder of place 637 in a time of 22 hours 53 minutes and 38 seconds to Iain Jackson eventual holder of place 688 in a time of 23 hours 4 minutes and 18 seconds. A gap of 11 minutes and thirty seconds in a twenty three hour event is not too shabby and I think we can safely say we finished as a team.

The great and the good of the Cally Challenge handed us those shiny foil blankets to keep us warm and parked us in a queue to wait for about twenty minutes to get a boat to the other side of the Loch where we could join John and catch some grub and apparently if the literature for the event were to be believed some free beer.

54 miles walked zero to go. No skin left on feet so can't have any blisters. Grub on board none but anticipated to be lots within the hour. Optimism replaced by relief. We had finished.

Party

After twenty minutes of contemplative huddling under a space blanket we were ushered out to the side of the Loch and hobbled our way into the waiting RIB. The boat driver clearly wanted to keep us awake and not only traversed the Loch at high speed but threw in a few fancy turns for good measure.

As we arrived at the far shore we truly knew we had finished. Tony almost got emotional. We stepped out of the boat and were presented with our gold finishing medals (aspiring Cally Challengers take note this is the best finishing medal I've had at any event and is almost worth keeping).

Almost the very next sight we were greeted by was a trouser less Paul who had just finished his recovery massage and was wandering back to the car. A pretty sight it was not but at least it was extremely recognisable and we followed him directly back to the waiting car rather than wandering the car park in aimless tired and fed up fashion looking for John.

Back at the car we all got fresh dry kit on and I removed my irksome boots for the last time ever. The next destination for the worthless leaking piece of crap that had masqueraded in Decathlon as a three season boot was the dustbin. I would have got blisters anyway, but soaking my feet in rain water for the first four hours of the event had absolutely made matters much worse.

Being members of the GWHSMWS the next destination was of course the free bar. I had been dreaming of a finishing pint for the last five miles and discussing it interminably with James who had repeatedly asserted he was sticking to water at the finish and taking the rehydration and recovery requirements seriously. Now he seemed to have changed his mind and led the charge (well OK hobble) down the slight hill to the free bar. The bar was empty. Not one single walker was availing themselves of free beer. Astonishing.

We availed ourselves of a free pint each and gratefully downed it, at a leisurely pace, though it took us at least five minutes to finish the first beer. A second beer was procured (for nothing) by Dickins, Jackson and Martin and we repaired to the breakfast tent. A fry up was the order of the day and when quizzed on our preferred choices of pig based produce we of course all chose large. Paul had the temerity to ask for a second fried egg which was greeted with a very gruff rebuff in fluent Glaswegian. Even I didn't catch exactly what he said but we all got the gist of it, I think his answer was no. Mind you if I had been up half the night cooking bacon and eggs for a bunch of smelly and

largely mono syllabic walkers I don't expect I would have been filled with the joys of spring either.
We chomped our way through as much food as the taciturn Glaswegian would serve us and finished our beers. It was time to head back to Fort William for much needed kip.
A quick check with John first though yielded the very welcome information that he was patient enough to wait whilst we got full value from the bar: Jackson, Martin and Dickins acquired a third beer and Pilcher and Kennedy a second. The literature we received before the event had missed a real trick and made very little of the free beer on offer. In fact the literature flew in the face of all reasonable judgement and actually downplayed the free beer, emphasising the vast amount of water needing to be drunk whilst hiking and that although free beer was on offer at the finish the average consumption was less than half a pint per walker. We managed by contrast a very respectable two and three fifths PPW (pints per walker). Heaven.
Now it was really time to head off though. It was now about 8:30am Sunday and we had risen at 5 am Saturday, and attractive as it was to continue to prop up the bar when the beer was free sleep was now becoming the pressing need.
Staying awake on the drive back to Fort William represented one of the harder bits of the challenge. John though was also pretty done in having got almost no sleep after he left us around check point four. Since I was sitting in the passenger seat next to him, and everyone in the back was asleep within two minutes of departure, I felt dropping off would not only be the height of bad manners but downright dangerous.
John had proved on multiple occasions in the last two days that he was nothing if not stoic and sticking to his task to

the end he drove steadily and safely the fifty miles back to Fort William.
On some very rare occasions I am quite glad that the label best fitting myself is *irascible pedant* and this was one of those rare occasions. There had been much email debate in the planning phase of this enterprise that we check out from Fort William on Saturday morning and check back in somewhere else Sunday afternoon thus saving one nights' accommodation cost. I had been equally insistent that we keep our Fort William hotel room for three nights since I didn't want to have to pack up at 6am Saturday morning but more importantly didn't want to wait for several hours to reach normal check in time in the early afternoon on Sunday. We got back to our hotel at 10:30'ish. If I had been faced with a three or four hour wait before I could lie down and sleep, I think I might have suffered a severe sense of humour failure. The walk upstairs to bed was tough enough, an hour and a bit in the car and I had seized like some one hundred year old car engine rusting away in a farmer's back yard for the last fifty years.
A proper clean up could wait for later. For now, sleep was the only thing on my mind. I laid down expecting to be asleep in seconds only to drift around in a semi sleep for quite a while. The body was exhausted, probably too tired to sleep, but the mind was still active. I drifted around in a state of semi consciousness for a while, just happy to be lying down, resting my aching feet and not hauling swarms of midges out of my ear. Paying for an extra night at the ridiculously cheap price of twenty seven pounds fifty was already worth every penny.
My next thought was waking after about six hours of the deepest, deep sleep. My ex Glaswegian boss would have described it not as sleep but a short session of death. It is

the feeling one rarely gets when rushing around in modern life. I didn't want to move an inch. I was awake but glued fast to the bed clothes with the duvet seamlessly wrapped around me creating a fug of warmth and comfort. After some minutes of simply lying there I discerned that James was already up and about but Paul, my other roomie for the trip, was still soundo.

I hobbled up and into the shower where the next twenty minutes was engaged in scrubbing off about three normal week's worth of grime and removing from my feet several yards of zinc oxide tape. Trust me for once in this missive I am not exaggerating there were literally yards of tape wound round my feet and once it was all removed it wasn't pretty. Aside from bruised toe nails (my big toe took exactly a year for the toe nail to return to normal), heel blisters, skinned toes and the usual war wounds I also had a huge patch of missing skin from the top of my left foot. Think of my foot as the British Isles then I was missing most of Wales and some of Scotland. Not nice.

I emptied most of a container of talc over other sore bits (no details use your imagination) got dressed in the practical and very stylish socks with sandals look and hobbled down stairs. It wasn't elegant, it was however a narrow winner over the old tramp wearing carpet slippers look that it had been in close competition with as one of the only two styles I could sport in my current condition.

I discovered James in the lounge of the hotel in the midst of a tea drinking marathon. Mark who looked exactly the same as usual had been out to buy the papers. Disappointingly GWHSMWS didn't feature in any of the sports pages. Obviously we finished too late for today's edition and would be reported at length in the Monday editions. More importantly Mark had researched local hostelries and had found a venue within walking distance (had to mean less than three hundred yards in current condition) that had big comfy seats and was showing Brazil vs. Australia in the World Cup with a five o'clock kick off. Just time to finish tea, round up everyone else and still get to the pub in time for a few beers before kickoff. Even better when the match finished a further two hundred yards down the road was a curry house where Martin and Jackson could reengage in their "Eat your own body weight in naan bread" competition. I couldn't have written the script better myself.

By virtue of the simple expedient of sitting still we very effectively rounded up the whole crew. Bit by bit everyone drifted into the lounge. John was tired but otherwise looked pretty normal. Tony was Ok (ish) as was James. Paul and I were in the worst shuffling tramp impersonation competition and Mark............. well Mark looked like he had just taken the dog for a stroll round the block. Bastard.

We walked/shuffled to the pub and five of us settled into very comfy seats in front of the wide screen. Mark to his credit set of as the most able bodied to make the first of what would be several trips to the bar. Whilst on many occasions my drink of choice would be a pint of fine real ale, Walworth's 6X is top choice but only if served in a pub with a six mile radius of Devizes, next on the list and a very different beer is Hartleys XB but only if served in Ulverston (I haven't been there for a few years and I'm not even sure if the brewery is still in Ulverston as it got bought a few years ago by some massive brewing company) and for a good traveller a pint of Adnams (bitter or broadside) will do nicely. On this occasion though there was only one possible drink that could fully revitalise my ailing constitution and that is the magic rehydration potion that is Stella Artois. I took a long draught of my first pint settled back to watch the footie and sent Mark off to get the next round in.

The footie was rather good actually. The soccerroos took no heed of the fact that they were there only to be the ritual whipping boys of the majestic Brazil and had a right good go at them. The first half was pretty even. Australia was well organised and efficient and apart from one delightful touch from (the otherwise fat and slightly useless) Ronaldo that nearly set up Kaka, Brazil didn't look like scoring.

Brazil scored a good first goal early in the second half courtesy of a final pass from a suspiciously offside Ronaldo to Adriano who finished well with the Aussie defence for once sleeping a bit. If I was facing a Brazilian with the ball at his feet twenty yards out I think I would be trying my damndest not to offer him one yard of space let alone the two the Aussies offered Adriano which was enough time to pull the ball back on to his left foot and enough space to

bury it in the bottom corner.
From then on it seemed to be pretty much all Aussie. They threw everything forward and really deserved a draw but in the end got caught on the break and first a ricochet from an Aussie defender fell straight at a Brazilians foot and then Robinho's shot screamed back of the post straight to Fred in a position from which even I could have scored from. (And yes he really is called Fred).
It was a bit harsh but a damn good crack watching the game. Mark meantime had elevated himself to God like status by being team fag the whole time and making numerous trips to the bar. Now I was rather grateful for his indestructibility and a little less jealous of his disappearing over the horizon on the occasion of every bit of uphill hiking.
I should really have kept score of our beer consumption but the nearest I could get to a quantitative assessment of beer intake was many. Now I ask you, devoted reader, what could possibly better to follow beer and footie than curry? Correct. There is nothing that better follows beer and footie than curry and by good fortune, or more probably resident enthusiast Tony, we had actually booked a table at the nearby curry restaurant.
The standard for curry ordering had long since been set by two of my fellow former rugby team mates, Serge and Podger. Serge earned his nickname after Serge Blanco, the elegant French full back. The common denominator with Matt Burnett aka "Serge" and Monsieur Blanco was the ability to kick a rugby football rather well with a bare foot (note this is not only the common denominator but the only single common characteristic of these two gentlemen).
Now Serge and Podger are not small chaps. Segre oscillated between a life as a full back and his more natural position

of prop. Podger played loose head prop, most of hooker and some of tight head prop all at the same time. Sometime late on a Saturday I stumbled on them enjoying their post match curry in a local restaurant. I don't remember exact details but their menu of choice ran something like main course chicken tikka for starter, followed by chicken vindaloo, side dish of main course size bomaby potato, onion bhaji, vegetable samosa, pilao rice, naan bread, and two chapattis. Each.

If you don't believe it is possible to consume these quantities, keep in mind that Podger once went to buy a round at the end of the annual rugby club supper and returned to the table of six with a bottle of port and a very large cigar. Each. (Not just a cigar each but also a bottle of port each. I promise you this is true).

I couldn't aspire to the Olympic standard curry consumption regularly displayed by Podger and Serge, but I could have a damn good go. For once in my life (and it isn't very often) I could without a pang of guilt and with a totally clear conscience eat exactly as much as it would take to be completely stuffed. Brilliant.

The curry was fantastic. Not quite as good as John's fried eggs I had eaten seemingly two lifetimes ago but right up there with the most satisfying grub ever consumed. We did get a bit told off from the waiters for being too rowdy, something we are also rather excellent at having imbibed too much alcohol. We stopped short of getting kicked out of the restaurant and backed off on volume a bit. Even in our current state it was not too difficult to understand the rest of the restaurant didn't want to share in our mixed emotions of celebration and relief. If any residents of Fort William reading this book remember their quiet Sunday evening curry being ruined by a bunch of noisy Southerners round

about mid 2006 I unreservedly apologise on behalf of my fellow whisky club members and myself.
Stuffed with so much curry that I now resembled an anaconda having swallowed a pig we waddled back to the hotel. Now the proper and sensible thing to do at his point would have been to go to bed. But we were neither proper nor sensible and considering all available choices we decided we ought to grace the hotel bar with the benefit of our custom and bought some more beers and some whisky chasers. At this point things start to get a bit hazy and difficult to recount in chronological order. So I will provide the list of activities for the rest of the evening as best I can and you can put them in any order you like, no one will doubt the veracity of your solution.

- John asks barman if it is OK if we drink fine bottle of very aged malt in his bar and borrows glasses for said purpose.
- Mark buys another round.
- Team presents Iain with fine bottle of very aged malt in recognition of organising training efforts.
- Mark buys another round.
- Iain retires to bed.
- Everyone has a look at the patch of skin missing from Iain's foot and feels ever so slightly sick.
- Tony retires to bed.
- Mark stays up all night to prove indestructibility and plans marathon run for next morning.
- Iain gets all tired and emotional after reading fine words written by Paul Martin in card attached to fine bottle of very aged malt.
- Mark buys another round.

- Everyone retires outside to get eaten alive by midges and smoke Paul Martin provided cigars.
- Mark buys another round.
- Crisps, peanuts and twiglets are bought (by Mark) and consumed gratuitously by Martin and Jackson.

Of course eventually even the best parties have to end. We had really hung it out as long as possible partly because we were on a high after finishing but mostly that this was the occasion when the walk itself was so strongly in our minds that we could really reflect on a job well done. With no little sadness, and an occasional burp, I dragged myself off to bed and drifted off for more part time death. Over. Now we really had finished.

Epilogue

I wondered a little bit as I was writing this what had the other guys made of it all. James had kept his own diary in the form of a series of sketches that are now the illustrations in this book. His last sketch was not so much a sketch as a series of random memories from the six months we had spent training and drinking together. I simply reproduce it here as his memories of the whole event. Paul had written some very nice words in a card presented to me during our finishing party that captured the essence of working as a team. We all had our ups and downs and

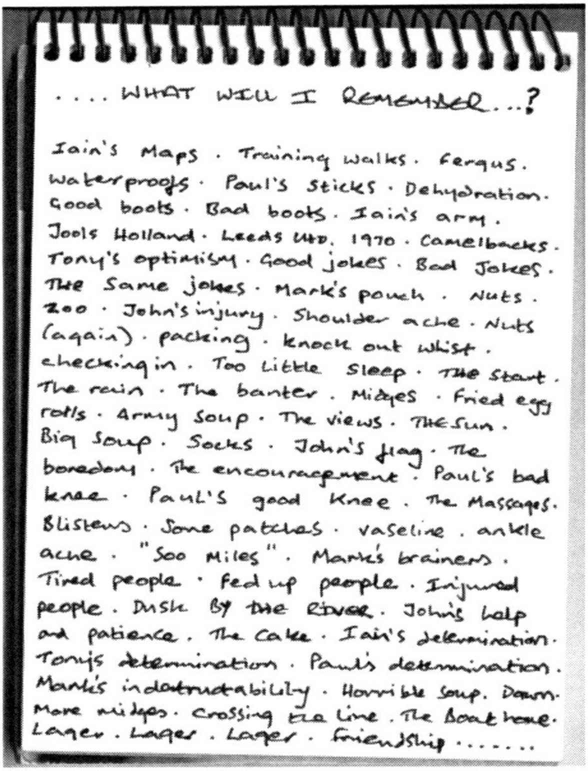

everyone (except Mark) had troughs when things didn't go so well. Feeling part of a team, sometimes support, sometimes peer pressure, sometimes sheer competitive bloody mindedness that meant you were not going to be the one to give up, had driven us on and helped us all finish. Still I felt the fellas all needed their say and I also wondered if any part of it was as fresh for them today as it had been for me writing this little tale. So in good whisky club fashion I would let them have their say and sent them an email.

> -----Original Message-----
> **From:** Iain Jackson
> **Sent:** 29 February 2008 08:32
> **To:** tony.kennedy; markdickins; James Pilcher; paul.martin; John Milner
> **Cc:** andy.parr
> **Subject:** Caledonian Challenge
>
> As some of you are aware I have been working on a book on our experiences training and completing the Cally Challenge. One thing I would like to fit in at the end reflecting on the whole experience is a few words from each of you on what the whole experience meant to you. Doesn't have to be long or meaningful it might have been nothing more than a long walk and a few beers and that is absolutely fine. My target is to fit in an email from each of you exactly as you write it without editing, (although it is of course also subject to the editorial influence of Mr. Parr who is helping review the material). No compulsion but if you would like to send me an email on what the CC meant for you I'll find it a space in my book.
> Iain

James
From: James Pilcher
Sent: den 6 mars 2008 18:31
To: Iain Jackson; tony kennedy; mark dickins; paul martin; John Milner
Cc: andy parr
Subject: RE: Caledonian Challenge

The Cally was simply one of the best things I have ever done. From a personal point of view I was really pleased that I finished within 24 hours, but the real blast was doing it with some good mates, with whom I had trained hard.
Particular highlights for me were...crossing the line with Iain, who managed to finish with me despite his feet being in a terrible mess....and the free lager tent at the end, where we studiously ignored all the health advice and got wasted – it was free what did they expect us to do ?!
I definitely want to go back and do it all again.... before my body says ..'stop doing these ridiculous things'...!
James

Tony
From: wendy kennedy]
Sent: den 26 mars 2008 20:55
To: Iain Jackson; 'mark dickins'; 'James Pilcher'; tony.kennedy; paul.martin; 'John Milner'
Cc: andy.parr
Subject: RE: Caledonian Challenge

So having conjured up a challenge late one whisky evening, did we remember the following days what we actually let ourselves in for.

It suddenly dawned on me i was about to take on one of the biggest challenges of my life.

Yes i have lots of energy and talk but would i actually make it to the end!!!

I have to say that those long training walks made me realise that this was not going to be a walk in the park and that to complete this challenge would
Take a miracle!!!

Actually it ended up being one of the most wonderful experiences I have ever been involved in, with a great bunch of friends and I still managed to talk until the last hour!!

I would not of made it round the course without all your support and encouragement

Thanks Guys
Tony

Mark

From: mark dickins [mailto:markdickins@hotmail.co.uk]
Sent: den 27 mars 2008 22:58
To: paul.martin; Iain Jackson
Cc: andy.parr; john milner; James Pilcher; Tony.Kennedy; wendy.Kennedy.co.uk
Subject: RE: Caledonian Challenge

So much to remember.
December - under-equipped, under-

prepared and 20 miserable miles in the freezing cold ....what were we embarking upon?!

June - eager anticipation as the last of the bags were crammed into Tony's car. Twelve hours of driving left me enough time to consume a Lance Armstrong autobiography that would hopefully inspire us through the 54 miles of unknown Scottish terrain.
Five hours sleep, a hearty breakfast and our arrival at a midge infested start with several hundred netted, cagouled, booted and rucksacked people. The adrenalin was pumping. All Iain's hard work in planning and training was now coming to fruition.
What a walk it was. I recall vast chunks of it vividly and with very fond memories, I can also recount the array of emotions that went with it!
There were soft pine laden tracks, boggy barren paths, rocky ascents, slippery descents, check point 2 that took forever to reach despite being visible for what appeared hours. The sun shone, it drizzled, it rained, it poured and Tony still managed to talk to every participant. Ludicrous conversations took place to shed the miles....and of course I wouldn't have used a bike had

one miraculously materialised and nobody had been watching! One was propelled to each check point by either the lure of food and refreshments prepared by 'Dad', the portoloos in Paul's case, or/and the massage that awaited to be delivered by a voluptuous blonde. (long walks do strange things to the mind)

The last 12 miles was covered predominately in the dark. Iain's feet were falling apart, Paul's knee had all but given up the ghost, there were a couple of sore nipples, a pair of bottoms that needed vaselining, there was a distinct lack of joviality and Tony had resorted to talking to himself, but I never doubted that we all would finish. I recall looking round at one point in those last few miles and seeing through the darkness a snaking trail of headlamps winding their way into the distance. We were part of this parade and it looked and felt fantastic.

Yes of course we all finished; in varying degrees of fatigue, approachability and well being, but after an hour and 3 free pints of Fosters we were all reliving and regaling stories of the past 24 hours.

I would simply like to thank Iain, James, Paul, Tony and John. Without all your help and support this wouldn't have been achievable. You were all superb. An

idea conceived out of a group of newly found friends sharing a 'small' glass of whisky....who would have believed it! It was a thrill, I have fantastic memories that will last a lifetime and fantastic friends that I hope will do likewise.
Mark

Paul

From: paul.martin
Sent: den 27 mars 2008 10:15
To: Iain Jackson
Cc: andy.parr; John Milner; James Pilcher; mark dickins; tony.kennedy
Subject: RE: Caledonian Challenge

As the Cally challenge escapade was driven off the back of the Whisky Club it is hard to separate the emotional ties to either ie each Whisky Club meeting generates as much excitement as does the approach to another annual challenge. The Cally stands-out because it our first "band of brothers" collective mid-life trial and so prepares the ground for later endeavours -and we all know that preparation is nine tenths of anything. The extension of the WMHSMC to include out-door pursuits not only panders to our competitive dispositions (overt or introvert) but is fundamental to the

dynamics of the club because it is easy to feel bonhomie at a Club meeting, especially as you descend into a fine malt induced stupor but it is not until a collective is stress tested that you really get to peer beneath that personal veneer of those around you and discover that you've just extended your family group. To stay with collective nouns the club would surely have remained any one of the following, a Babble, or a Shuffle or even a Bellowing but what we have ended up with is a Pride or a Fellowship - if that's not a little too Independence Day.
My recollections of the day is that it was a journey of physical and mental discovery completed in a 21 hour period over spectacular Scottish countryside. My only regret is that we started together and for the majority of the challenge we stayed together but at the end the pain in my knee (motor bike induced arthritis) meant that i was not very sociable and i passed anonymously over the finishing line. In hind sight, i feel sad about that and would like an opportunity to put it right although i fear a moment passed is a moment lost - still on to the next challenge.

Paul Martin
Charles Taylor Consulting

John
From: John Milner
Sent: den 25 mars 2008 22:09
To: Iain Jackson
Cc: andy.parr; markdickins; James Pilcher; tony.kennedy; paul.martin
Subject: RE: Caledonian Challenge

Sorry for delay

Having enjoyed the training walks so much particularly watching some of the harder but initially ill equipped members of our team freezing their nads off on the the artic Thames Marshes in winter it was a bitter sweet experience to get injured. Sweet knowing that I wouldn't have to do the f****g thing but bitter knowing that I could have and should have.**

So the drop into support driver role was second best but still great to be part of the whole shooting match. My team treated me like a walker and I did actually walk a bit of the route with between checkpoint 2 and 3. Walking back against the flow could have provided a chapter on body language and the path to success or failure.

I performed a number of roles. Midge swatter at the start, café proprietor at checkpoint 1, sock drier and cajoler of men thinking they weren't hungry at checkpoint 2, concerned parent losing touch with their errant teenagers at checkpoint 3, MASH type medic at checkpoint 4 and spaced out hippie at the finish.

A fantastic event that I will complete and hopefully my feet won't end up as bad as Iain's and I will be less grumpy than Paul. I'm also planning to spend a pre-event week training with SAS Mark and a week

living at Tony's house to soak up that optimism. I might even do a week's art class with James to round the whole thing off.

cheers

John Milner APMP MRICS
Member
For and on behalf of Baily Garner LLP
www.bailygarner.co.uk

And last from Wendy (Tony's wife)
From: wendy kennedy
Sent: den 27 mars 2008 22:46
To: Iain Jackson
Subject: RE: Caledonian Challenge

Ian,
As you know due to lack of computer nous Tony and I continue to share our email access which means I chuckle along with the boy talk!
Would your best seller benefit from a wife's perspective?
I would have to tell you that in 20 yrs of marriage that was the only the second occasion when I have been worried enough about Tony to lose sleep worrying about his safety.
Aside from the obvious danger I was also concerned that Tony's optimism would put him at risk of physical injury from a team member after the first 12 hours
I spent a sleepless night expecting a call from mountain rescue at any moment.
By 5am when no call had arrived I got up and I am ashamed to admit I sat in front of the computer awaiting news.
Rgds
Wendy

So what next? We continue to enjoy our outdoor training and occasional events. 2007 saw the same group plus two more mountain biking round and climbing up Snowdon. 2008 sees us planning and entered for Vatternrundan a 300km bike ride round a Swedish lake. We're even in planning mode for an ambitious assault in 2009. Most of us were having dinner at Paul's as a surprise birthday party for Christine, James's wife. Somehow the conversation turned to the topic of sailing and the Isle of White "Round the Island Race". A few us (well two actually Wendy, Tony's wife, and me) had sailed before and before long the red wine did its work and the plan was set. Round the Island race 2009, two boats, whisky club chaps vs. whisky club ladies now that really would be a challenge!
The Cally Challenge is something we will return to though 2010, or maybe when we can muster an average age over fifty, one way or another we will be back.
The kind of endeavour exemplified by the Cally Challenge is never as hard as you think.
Malcolm Wilden, the former first team captain at Gravesend, said many wise things on the subject of rugby but the one that still sticks in my mind was approximately the following. "It doesn't matter how cold and dark it is, or how hard the training is, the hardest part of rugby training on a winters evening is to pick up your kit bag and open the front door."

So why not pick up your literal or metaphorical kit bag and give it a go, you never know you might even enjoy it.

Glossary of terms

Blister Seemingly insignificant fluid filled swelling of the skin. Usually brought upon by friction or heat. Can turn nasty, beware.

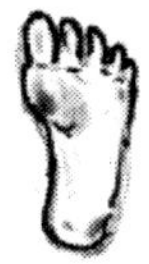

BMB Beardy Munro Bagger. (See Munro) Individual who spends life ticking of the 284 summits that make the complete list of the Munros. Always wears a beard.

Bollocksed Mild state of incapacity often through the taking of excess drink.

Cigar Cylindrical tobacco objects at least 8 inches in length and 1 inch in diameter. Allegedly to be enjoyed by setting fire to it and inhaling resulting smoke cloud. Much beloved by Paul Martin.

Confit (of duck) Method of cooking duck involving first boiling the duck to render the fat and then roasting the duck in the resulting fat. The tray of hot duck and fat needs to be handled with extreme caution.

Dickens Charles 19th century author and some time resident of Kent. Not to be confused with Dickins (see below)

Dickins Mark Annoyingly gifted natural athlete, aka bastard especially when cycling/running/walking miles in front without breaking sweat. Not to be confused with Dickens (see above)

Dram Scottish measure of whisky. If poured at home can be assumed to be roughly half a pint.

E9 7a Rock climbing grade in ordinary language; equates to impossible.

Enthusiast See Tony

Fatlete Term for fat person attempting some kind of ridiculous athletic endeavour. Resulting athletic endeavors usually highly embarrassing.

Fergus Dog with no brain at all. See also Wheaten Terrier

Footle (r) (ing) See Phaff

Force five Reference to Beaufort scale measurement of wind speed.

Formula one Not to be confused with the over hyped over paid intensely dull sport conceived by Bernie Ecclestone for the single purpose of pulling attractive girl friends. No this is an extremely stupid 100 year old board game beloved by James Pilcher.

Gaffer Tape Industrial strength silver tape usually used for air conditioning assembly. Can also be used for foot repair and nipple rub prevention.

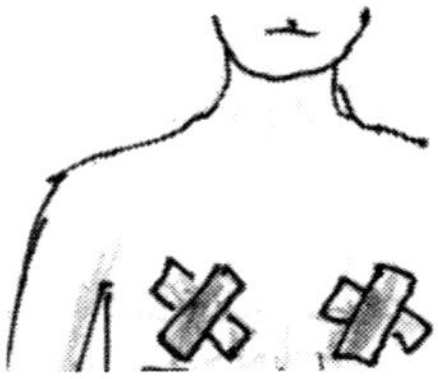

Gravesend Eponymous Kentish town located at what was once the end of the estate of the Earl of Gravesham. Alternative sources for naming the town include the apocryphal story its name is derived from the location where bodies from the Black Death thrown in the Thames were washed ashore. A tiny bit famous for being something to do with Pocahontas.

Irascible Pedant Grumpy bad tempered creature known for repeatedly stating opinions as facts, mostly rubbish opinions. Refuses to be swayed from stated facts (i.e. opinions) even in the face of overwhelming evidence to the contrary. Best avoided at all times. See also Jacko.

Jacko

Irascible pedant and fatlete useful only for high speed beer drinking and snoring. See http://www.caledonianchallenge.com/past/gallery06.php and look for reference 384 for Jacko based photography. (The one lying down not the pretty one standing up).

Malt whisky

Whisky produced from a single distillery with malted barley. Impossible to find a bad one.

MBHO

Management by hopeful outcome. Delusional management technique involving a belief system based on the false premise that simply stating what you would have as a perfect outcome will actually change anything.

Midge

Small insect prevalent in all parts of Scotland. Appears in vast numbers in the wrong weather conditions. Has reportedly caused English campers

unaware of the beast's voracious appetite to go insane. See www.highland-midge.co.uk for more details.

Mirauculous *(Pron: Mi-rauk-u-lous)* Scottish term for severe incapacity resulting from the taking of vast excess of drink. As in: *He was completely mirauculous.*

Munro Scottish mountain over 3000 feet high

Optimist See Tony

Phaff (er) (ing) Severe procrastination brought upon by the incapacity to make the simplest decision without at least twenty minutes bag sorting. See also footle.

Racing snake Extremely fit fast ascender of mountains (see BMB).

Rugby Union The best sport in the world

SSOD Short session of death: Unconscious sleep usually following a state best described by mirauculous (see mirauculous) or tired (see tired).

Stampsies Entertaining variation on conkers where participants are legitimately allowed to tread fiercely on an opposition conker should it accidently land on the floor.

Stella Artois Secret training juice of GWHSMWS. Six pints guarantees complete rehydration after even the most strenuous of workouts.

Stocious *(pron: Stow-sh-us)* As per mirauculous

Tired A physical sate reached by staying up for 27 hours during which time you walk 54 miles and then drink three pints of lager.

Tony Personification of optimism and enthusiasm. Remains optimistic in the face of incontrovertible evidence to the contrary.

TTC The Third Choice. Delusional management technique where management imagines that when faced with two difficult choices creating an unrealistic third choice that is impossible to achieve has actually changed something.

V diff Climbing term meaning very difficult. Equates for real climbers to trivially easy.

The Windmill With due mention to The Cock at Luddesdowne the best pub in the world (or at least in East Kent)

Wheaten terrier Breed of dog. Skittish hyperactive brainless species suited only to ratting and barking.

Whisky The best drink in the world.

Zinc oxide tape (Military strength) Breathable adhesive tape used for holding surgical dressings in place. In extreme can also be used in vain attempt to prevent blisters (see gaffer tape).

LaVergne, TN USA
04 August 2010
192019LV00002B/8/P

9 781899 820542